Beginner's Guide
Special Education

D0893051

3

4

Preface

This book is aimed at those teachers who are in training or are new to teaching. It will also be of interest to anyone who wants an introduction to learning how pupils with special educational needs can be taught in mainstream primary and secondary schools.

The first two chapters explain the legislative context and procedures linked to the Code of Practice. The next looks in some depth at the principles of differentiation.

Chapter 4, written by Mike Murphy uses his recent experiences as a secondary school special educational needs co-ordinator and deputy head teacher, to investigate ways to match teaching and learning styles.

The remaining chapters examine in turn, the use of support assistants and support services, working with pupils and parents and keeping good records. The final chapter discusses issues of inclusive practice.

Chapter 1
What is meant by a special educational need?

The purpose of this chapter is to introduce the concept of special educational needs and the relevant recent legislation.

The definition

The term 'special educational needs (SEN)' came into being with the 1981 Education Act, replacing the previous list of disabilities of mind and body used in the 1944 Act. The 1981 Act stated that:

A child has a special education need if she or he has a learning difficulty which calls for special educational needs provision to be made for him or her. A child has a learning difficulty if he or she:

- has a significantly greater difficulty in learning than the majority of children of the same age, or
- has a disability which prevents or hinders the child from making use of educational facilities of the kind provided for children of the same age in schools within the area of the Local Education Authority (LEA).

This same definition of special educational needs was used in the 1993 and 1996 Education Acts. It was also made clear that those who speak an alternative language at home shall not be included in the category of SEN for this reason alone.

The shift away from using the 'medical' definitions of the 1944 Act meant it was possible to develop a more interactive model of SEN; one that recognised that the 'within child' factors were not the sole reason for difficulties. The curriculum on offer and the environment of a school could now be considered part of the reason the pupil had difficulties in learning.

The definition in the 1981 Act could also mean that a pupil might be perceived as having significant difficulties in one setting, but not in another, because of the relativity to the peer group. It must be remembered that the term SEN was meant to describe pupils whose needs are persistent and long term.

The Warnock Report (DES, 1978) had suggested that one child in six might at some time in their school career have a special educational need. The 1981 Act endeavoured to indicate that there would be a continuum of need for those with short-term problems to those with long-term and complex difficulties. In recent years, between 2 - 4 per cent of pupils in each LEA have Statements of SEN indicating a significant degree of difficulty or disability and upwards of 18 per cent may be identified as having some level of SEN requiring extra support in school.

Children Act 1989

This act emphasises the rights of children to be listened to when decisions are being made which will affect them. While not having education as its focus, being concerned mainly with situations where Social Services or the law are involved, the Children Act influenced the thinking of those drawing up the first Code of Practice (1994).

The Code of Practice (DfE, 1994)

The *Code of Practice on the Identification and Assessment of Special Education Needs* (DfE, 1994) is a Government document explaining how identification and assessment of special educational needs should be carried out by schools and LEAs. The status of the Code is a document that schools and LEAs should 'have regard to'. Most of the content is advisory, although certain parts are regulations and therefore legal requirements.

The principles of the Code of Practice are that:

- the needs of all pupils with SEN should be addressed. The Code recognises that there is a continuum of needs and provision which will be made in a wide variety of forms;
- children with SEN should have the greatest possible access to a broad and balanced education including the National Curriculum;
- for the majority of pupils, identification and assessment and subsequent provision for SEN will be the responsibility of the school.

The SEN Tribunal

The SEN Tribunal was set up by the Education Act 1993. It considers parents' appeals against decisions by the LEA about a child's special educational needs, where the parents cannot reach agreement with the LEA over the Statementing process.

Roles and responsibilities

The Code of Practice describes the various responsibilities for SEN in mainstream schools. The overall responsibility for these pupils lies with the governors and head teacher but all teachers have responsibility for those pupils in their classes with SEN, and parents, pupils and ancillary staff have their roles to play. The co-ordination of the day-to-day policy and practice for SEN is the responsibility of the special educational needs co-ordinator (SENCO).

It is important to remember that everyone has a role to play in what is known as a 'whole-school approach' to meeting SEN. All must have regard to the Code of Practice when carrying out their duties towards pupils with SEN. Everyone must have regard also to their own school's SEN Policy. School policies should also state the name of the school's SENCO.

A SENCO in a primary school may be a class teacher who takes on this additional responsibility, but the role could be given to the deputy head or the head teacher or to teachers with other additional responsibilities. Some may be part-time, not class-based but often offering support as part of their role. All SENCOs keep the SEN Register up to date and advise colleagues in writing and reviewing IEPs. The time given to SENCOs varies enormously, particularly in primary schools. In secondary schools the SEN co-ordination is more often a full-time role in its own right or that of a learning support department.

Whole-school approach

All schools are required to have a whole-school policy for SEN, on which they report annually to parents. This should include a description of 'how resources are allocated to and amongst the pupils with SEN'. Effective schools manage special educational needs by being clear about their priorities when allocating roles and responsibilities. Effective school policies also depend on good communication systems between all those holding these responsibilities. The school moves forward in its development by integrating special needs policies into the school development as a whole. Often what is good practice for SEN is good practice for all. School SEN policies should include information about how children with SEN are integrated within the school as a whole, and what arrangements are made to provide access to a balanced and broadly based curriculum including the National Curriculum.

Local Education Authorities' responsibilities

It is the duty of LEAs, under the Education Act 1996, to keep under review all their arrangements for SEN provision and to inform governing bodies of the schools in their area of such arrangements. The LEA can request help from any District Health Authority and Social Service Department in the executions of its duties towards children with SEN and, provided those requests are reasonable, they must comply. LEAs are responsible for all children in their area, who are educated at maintained schools or at independent schools at the expense of the authority, and those at non-maintained or independent schools whose needs have been brought to their attention by parents.

OFSTED Reports on the Code of Practice (1994)

OFSTED/HMI have monitored the implementation of the Code of Practice each year by surveying schools of different types and in different LEAs. These surveys all confirm that progress was being made in implementing the Code of Practice in most schools, that the Code has helped schools match provision to needs and that they were more successful in identifying pupils' learning and behavioural problems.

The latest HMI report (1999) focused on the contribution made by the Individual Education Plan (IEP) to raising standards for pupils with SEN. This survey found that pupils' views were rarely sought in the preparation of IEPs. This survey also noted that many LEAs had little or no specialist support at Stage 3 from the LEA's support services.

The report concluded by stating that 'the principal purpose of an IEP is to clarify what is to be done in the immediate short term to help the pupil and staff to enable the pupil to make progress'. IEPs were most likely to be effective when they were part of the school's overall arrangements for assessment and recording (see further information in Chapter 2).

The National Curriculum

All pupils with SEN, whether they have a Statement or not, are entitled to the full National Curriculum, unless an exemption is spelled out in the child's Statement. National Curriculum assessments and tests, along with other teacher observations, may help identify pupils with SEN.

Teachers may also be alerted to specific learning difficulties when there is a significant difference in attainments between one core subject and another, for example when reading standards are much lower than those in mathematics and science.

The curriculum is the context for learning in schools. Planning is needed, therefore, to help all pupils overcome potential barriers to learning. This planning will include the adaptation of tasks, materials and the learning environment.

These potential barriers will differ for individuals and groups of pupils. It will be important to use information gained from assessing the types of barriers to learning that occur in your class, to inform your curriculum planning, both in the long and short terms. For example, for those with communication and literacy difficulties, it will be necessary to use texts that pupils can read and understand. Using Information and Communications Technology (ICT) and other aids such as taped material will increase access for many pupils. For others, using visual clues or signs and symbols will help communication.

For those with emotional barriers to learning, it will help to identify those aspects with which the pupils can engage. Positive feedback will be helpful to reinforce learning and build self-esteem. Allowing time for pupils to engage in learning will be important. Many pupils find time a problem. Many work at a very slow pace, so it will be important to organise time for a proportion of work to be finished. Curriculum differentiation will be discussed in more depth in Chapters 3 and 4.

Inclusion Statement

The Revised National Curriculum (2000) has eight pages known as the Inclusion Statement. This makes clear that schools should vary the delivery of the curriculum so that all pupils may have access to its content assessment.

The first parts of this statement encourage schools to be flexible about teaching to allow for differences of gender, ethnicity, culture and language. The last part explains how those with disabilities should be catered for by specific additional equipment, techniques or support.

The Green Paper and the Programme for Action

In 1997 the Government published a Green Paper called 'Excellence for All'. The paper outlined ideas for further developments in inclusive education for those with SEN. At the end of 1998, after the consultation phase ended, an action plan was published outlining Government intentions to implement its policies.

The Programme for Action (DfEE, 1998a) put forward Government policies which it was hoped would improve the following areas:

- working with parents to achieve excellence for all;
- improving the SEN Framework – this will mean introducing a new Code of Practice in 2001 – improving IEPs and improving the effectiveness of the SEN Tribunal;
- developing a more inclusive education system;
- increased opportunities for staff development to include Learning Support Assistants (LSAs) and teachers;
- improving the way LEAs and other agencies work together to support children with SEN.

Code of Practice Revision (Consultation Document 2000)

A draft version of the revised Code went to consultation in the summer of 2000. It is hoped that the final version will be in place in 2001, though this may be delayed to take account of new legislation (SEN Disability Rights in Education Bill), also in consultation in 2000.

The principles of the revised Code of Practice remain the same. However, it begins with two new chapters emphasising the importance of parent partnership and of listening to and taking account of the pupils' views and perspectives. The chapter on parent partnership emphasises the role played by parent partnership schemes to be set up by all LEAs in offering consultation services. It is hoped this will reduce the number of SEN Tribunal cases.

The advice to schools is divided into phase sections; Early Years, Primary and Secondary. There is a change in emphasis, removing the five-staged approach of the 1994 Code and replacing it with what is called a graduated response, comprising two school-based stages. The implication is that all but exceptional cases will be met by these stages to be called either School Action or School Action Plus. At the same time as the publication of the draft Code, revised versions of some regulations were also published. There was also an appendix to the Code giving descriptions and examples of cases of different types of difficulties, to help decisions about the thresholds between the new stages.

Chapter 2
Identification and assessment

Identification of those with SEN

A first step in helping those with special needs is to make a decision about which children could be described as having sufficient need to be placed on the school's SEN register (Code of Practice, 1994). All children have individual needs, but these are not necessarily related to learning difficulties or disabilities as defined by the Code of Practice. Teachers' concerns usually centre around the pupils' lack of progress in one or more aspects of learning or their behaviour in class.

To warrant a description of SEN, a child should have learning difficulties which have been causing concern over time, probably to both parents and teachers, so there has to be the notion of significant sustained difficulties. Such a child is not responding as expected to the curriculum on offer, or cannot cope within the normal classroom environment without additional help.

However, the Code of Practice encourages all class teachers to register any of their concerns or those of parents by discussing these with the school's SENCO who will offer advice on how support can be given.

The next step will be to collect information about the pupil. This will include parents' views and the child's own perception of their learning, as well as evidence from previous records. Observation of the child within the class situation may reveal contextual reasons for the difficulty. Relationships within school need to be examined, between child and teacher and child and other children.

SENCOs have the responsibility of maintaining the school's record of pupils with SEN. For pupils thus identified, information gathering and assessment takes place, and this information contributes to individual or class teaching plans aimed at reducing the pupil's learning difficulties. SENCOs have a major role in advising and supporting staff over such planning. The planning will include both deciding on classroom management and curriculum differentiation as well as designing Individual Education Plans.

Early Years Settings

The Revised Code advises the appointment of a SENCO to be shared by groups of early years providers. Their role is to ensure liaison with parents and professionals and to advise and support other practitioners ensuring that IEPs are in place and targets set.

A graduated response

The Revised Code replaces the 1994 Code of Practice five-staged approach with what is called a graduated response. It is assumed that normal assessment and recording procedures will ensure identification of those whose progress is a cause for concern, which will be notified to parents usually by the SENCO. Careful records of action taken replaces Stage 1 of the original Code.

After a period of time each child's progress should be reviewed, and if it is considered necessary, extra school-based support be given along with more detailed planning carried out through the IEP. This stage will be called School Action in the Revised Code. A few pupils may require the help of outside support services and agencies, called School Action Plus in the Revised Code. Many children with recognised physical and sensory disabilities, those with more severe learning difficulties along with those with speech and language difficulties or those on the autistic spectrum, will have been assessed pre-school and will already be known to outside agencies or have a Statement on entering school. Regular review of progress for those pupils defined as having SEN is essential. Most pupils will remain on school-based stages until their needs are met. For those whose needs are greater, review is also important to monitor progress and revise plans and resources.

The same concept of a graduated response is advised for the Foundation Stage (ages 3-5). The Early Learning Goals are to guide expectations, but there is a reminder that there will be a variety of reasons for different rates of progress, not all indicating a special need.

The Individual Education Plan

For these children who have extra requirements, planning is needed, in order to 'fine tune' the programme of teaching and support more precisely. This requires a much more specialised form of planning known as an Individual Education Plan (IEP) (see Figure 1).

Figure 1 - Individual Education Plan

Child's name .... Date of birth .... NC Year .... COP stage ....

Date of plan .... Plan number .... External Specialist Support (if available) ....

Pupil's strengths and attainments	Areas of concern	
Pupil views	Parent views/role	
Pastoral and medical requirements		

Learning Targets [state these precisely]	Teaching Strategies [frequency of support]	How progress will be assessed and monitored

Review outcomes

Teacher's name

Date of IEP Review or Annual Review

....

15

An Individual Education Plan includes information about the nature of the child's learning difficulties.

- action – the special educational provision;
  - staff involved, including frequency of support;
  - specific programmes/activities/materials/equipment;
- help from parents at home;
- targets to be achieved in a given time;
- any pastoral care or medical requirements;
- monitoring and assessment arrangements;
- review arrangements and date.

Additionally for Stage 3:
Further advice from other agencies to draw up a new Individual Education Plan, including the involvement of support services (Code of Practice 1994, para. 2:93, 2.105).

The Revised Code emphasises that three to four 'crisp' targets should be written to represent a range of a pupil's priority needs across key curriculum areas.

Information that was initially collected about concerns and all baseline or standard assessments will be used in the IEP. Information about the pupil's strengths and interests should also be recorded. This is important, because it is through these strengths that positive progress will be made. Pupils' views must be sought as well as those of parents. The purpose of an IEP is to collate information which in turn will give ideas as to how best to teach the pupil and develop a plan of action, with targets that can be understood and achieved by the pupil and his/her teachers and parents. It must be accessible to everyone as a working document which will influence classroom practice. It has to be specific and achievable, but must also be feasible to use in ordinary classrooms. Basic information from each IEP must be given to all teachers who may teach the pupil. This is on a 'need to know' basis, so that the information is read and used.

Reviewing of Individual Education Plans
The purpose of IEPs is to improve record-keeping and planning which will make monitoring the progress of all pupils with SEN more effective. To ensure such monitoring is regular and informative, every pupil on

School Action or School Action Plus, must have a regular review of their progress and a revision of their IEP to meet any newly identified needs. This review process is the key to successful SEN management.

The class teacher in primary schools will often review IEPs but should remember to include parent and pupil views. It may, however, be better if colleagues work together in year groups to review. Review practice in secondary schools varies a great deal. It is advisable for the SENCO not to attempt to review all those with IEPs, but to establish an effective way to ensure the reviews are carried out regularly. This might be done by involving form tutors and year heads in the process. A planned timetable for IEP reviews is needed for every school. Time is such a scarce resource that it must be allocated formally for this process. It is a role for senior management to both allocate and safeguard this time for IEP reviews.

The SENCO may be involved in setting up the review process, acting as a consultant to colleagues and helping in decision-making for those pupils for whom it is necessary to move to a different stage. It must be remembered that many children's needs will be fully met after some help has been given. For these children IEPs would be discontinued.

It must be known which pupils have significant needs that affect their progress in one or more aspects of the curriculum and will require a specialised and supported programme written on their IEP. The resource implications must be considered.

School Action Plus

For those pupils who need additional support or advice, it is likely that a great deal of assessment will already have taken place. There will have been a working IEP for at least two to four terms and the pupil's learning styles and difficulties will be well known. Such pupils will be causing additional concern, because they are still not making expected progress. It is for this reason that outside agencies, in particular support services, such as learning support teachers or educational psychologists, are called in to add their views. They add to the assessment information by carrying out a range of tests or observations, or by working closely with the pupil and listening to their perspective (see Chapter 6).

If the advice is to move to School Action Plus, then the purpose of the outsider's assessment is to advise on the IEP for the pupil. Parents must also be informed and given opportunities to help set targets.

The number of pupils at this stage may be limited by the availability of local support services. This varies considerably across the country. An IEP could continue to be important for some pupils throughout much of their school life.

LEA-based stages

Some children have disabilities or learning difficulties that are significant enough to warrant additional resources and support provided by the LEA. If it is thought that this might be the case, teachers and parents, through the school, may ask the LEA to assess these needs. For those few pupils whose needs justify further formal assessment, careful and detailed documentation will be needed about their problems and how these have been met to date. At the review, where a multi-disciplinary assessment is being considered, parents' views must be sought. After all the advice from everyone who knows the child, including the parents, has been considered, the LEA may decide to issue a Statement (or Record of Need in Scotland). The possibility that the LEA, a) may not agree to the assessment, or, b) may not issue a Statement, must be explained, along with the parents' right to appeal.

Thresholds

The Revised Code has an Appendix section describing the triggers or thresholds for deciding to move a pupil to School Action *or* for those requiring further assessment from outside agencies. The case studies are used to illustrate these triggers.

Most LEAs have set quite stringent criteria for statutory assessments which they will have published. LEAs often have standard forms they wish schools to complete when requesting a formal assessment. The Code of Practice states very clearly that it is the head teacher's responsibility to make the decision to request a formal assessment, unless a parent has already done so. This is, however, usually done in close co-operation with the SENCO. The SENCO will then be asked to collect and collate all documentation, IEPs and supporting evidence and either they or the head will write to the LEA making a formal request for further assessment. If the LEA agrees to proceed with this assessment, schools will be asked to write a report about the child, which becomes advice attached as final documentation of the Statement. Parents' views are similarly attached.

Making a formal assessment

If the LEA agrees to the assessment they have a duty under the Code to carry this out within six months. This may or may not result in a decision by the LEA to give a Statement. If the LEA wishes, they can write a 'note in lieu' of a Statement, which means the pupil's needs continue to be met at School Action Plus. Statements can be issued with or without resources. A draft Statement, written using the evidence from all these reports, is sent to the parent who may ask for changes to be made. If the LEA and the parent cannot agree to these changes or there is a dispute over placement decisions, the parent may take the matter to the SEN Tribunal. But first, most LEAs will attempt to mediate a mutually satisfactory solution to the parents' request, possibly using the parent partnership officer.

What is a Statement?

A Statement is a record of the child's needs, and it sets out the targets which would be appropriate to aim at in the immediate future. It also sets out the extra provision which the LEA is suggesting as appropriate. This could be extra or specialist teaching, specific programmes to meet the therapeutic needs or specific strategies which teachers could employ.

Attached to the Statement are copies of all the pieces of advice collected during the assessment process. These must be from the parent, the school, the educational psychologist and the health service and may be from others, if appropriate. The Statement is reviewed annually by the school who suggest to the LEA any significant changes that need to be made. Parents are always invited to attend Annual Reviews and their views recorded.

Pupils with Statements

Pupils with Statements in mainstream schools follow the normal programmes of study, but may have additional programmes to meet their needs. Many have either a support assistant or a support teacher for limited periods, to help them access the curriculum. Any specific therapy treatments or technical aids are also listed in the Statement. IEP planning continues with short-term targets set by the school and any relevant outside agencies. Each pupil with a Statement has a review annually, to determine whether the Statement is still needed and, if so, whether it needs to be changed in any way. Changes to the Statement are the LEA's responsibility once the report from the Annual Review is received from the school.

A very few pupils with Statements may go to special classes or special schools. They too follow modified programmes of study within the National Curriculum. They may be taught by specialist teachers and may have considerable input from therapists who visit some special schools regularly.

Types of special educational need

The majority of pupils can have their needs met within the normal curriculum. Schools now carry out a great deal of assessment within the National Curriculum arrangements and the programmes of study help

19

teachers to structure their teaching by progression through a planned curriculum. However, for children identified as having SEN, further individual assessments will be necessary.

Although the 1981 Act tried to get away from labels related to medical descriptions, the Code of Practice described different types of SEN using impairment definitions. Such definitions can be useful, but only if they lead to decisions about how to assess and teach the pupil. It is also important to remember that some pupils will not fit neatly within a single definition. (More information on each of these definitions can be found in the NASEN Spotlight series.)

Below are some general descriptions of typical definitions of disabilities. However, it is important to remember that it is essential to assess each child's needs individually. If those needs are considerable it is likely that multi-professional assessment will have taken place which will give extra individual information.

Continuum of need

It is also important to remember the concept of the 'continuum of need'. This term describes the range of disability from mild or moderate to severe and complex. The most complex needs are almost always multiple in nature involving many kinds of difficulty, possibly affecting communication, learning and mobility.

The Revised Code of Practice Appendix suggests four main categories for explaining the types of SEN. These will be used below to group the definitions; however, the points made above about overlap of needs still applies.

Cognition and learning difficulties

General learning difficulties is a description that covers pupils who appear not to be coping with most programmes of study relevant to the Key Stage appropriate to his/her age. The description includes those children who are working significantly below their contemporaries in the same subjects and who are falling progressively behind the majority of children of their age.

This group of pupils covers a wide range of ability, from those whose difficulties are mild or moderate to those whose are profound, multiple and complex.

The provision made for those whose difficulties are mild to moderate may well be able to be delivered in a mainstream setting. It is more likely that those with severe and complex learning difficulties will attend a special school or class.

Pupils with general learning difficulties may need to work at a different pace from others. Often a small-step approach is recommended for those learning targets chosen on the IEP.

Specific learning difficulties or dyslexia
This description covers children who only have difficulties related to reading, writing, spelling or manipulating numbers. They may be able to demonstrate an average or high level of ability orally. Such children can be severely frustrated and may also have developed emotional barriers to learning.

The British Psychological Society's definition of dyslexia is that 'Dyslexia is evident when accurate and fluent word reading and/or spelling develops very incompletely or with great difficulty. This implies that the problem is severe and persistent despite appropriate learning opportunities. It provides a basis for a staged approach of assessment through teaching' (DECP, 1999).

Structured programmes for reading, spelling and sometimes mathematical computation will need to be offered. Alternative approaches to recording work should be available so that pupils can demonstrate their conceptual understanding of other subjects. Multi-sensory approaches are most appropriate for this group (see Chapter 4).

Communication and interaction
The speech and language difficulties or delay of some pupils may have been identified pre-school. These children will typically have a short attention span, difficulty in either comprehending spoken language and/or expressing themselves coherently. Some pupils may have suffered a hearing impairment which could co-exist or be the cause of speech and language problems.

Children with language difficulties may exhibit behaviour that can be misunderstood. Listening involves selective attention, but those with language difficulties may not have this ability and are easily distracted.

It is important to make sure such pupils understand instructions by repeating these personally to the child and checking understanding regularly. Some children with speech and language difficulties will have a special programme devised by speech therapists.

Autistic spectrum disorder (ASD)
Autism can be described as a disability affecting the development of communication and social interaction. It is often characterised by the rigid

behaviours which children display due to the impairment of thought processes. Seach (1998) says that all those with an autistic spectrum disorder will display the 'Triad of Impairments' consisting of impairment in:

- social interaction;
- social communication;
- thought and imagination.

There is no one pattern of learning and teaching that works for every child. Children with ASD like routines that help them to understand what is expected of them. Routines can be used as starting points to introduce new skills. Giving clear instructions possibly using symbols to clarify meaning will aid understanding.

Emotional, behavioural and social difficulties
Some pupils' difficulties in learning are caused by their emotional state or by their inability to acquire appropriate learning behaviour. Pupils may be continually off-task, sometimes disrupting others, sometimes only themselves. Such pupils often have low self-esteem and poor learning strategies.

It is important to have high expectations of pupils with emotional and behavioural difficulties and ensure that they take part in class activities and are given full opportunity to learn and make progress. Extra care will be necessary to see that work is suitably planned, often using a small-step approach to enable success.

Pupils at risk of exclusion
A few pupils may be at serious risk of permanent exclusion when their behaviour is deteriorating rapidly. Such pupils may already have had some temporary exclusions.

Circular 10/99 suggests that young people at risk of permanent exclusion will need a Pastoral Support Programme (PSP) which is school-based but set up in conjunction with other agencies including the LEA. Where a pupil already has an IEP in place this should incorporate the approaches of the PSP.

The PSP will need to be agreed with parents who should be regularly informed about their child's progress. The school should invite the parents and an LEA representative to discuss areas of concern and what can be reasonably required of the pupil. The LEA should help monitor and support the plan. Other agencies such as social services, housing, careers and voluntary or community groups may be involved. It will be important to link the PSP with the IEP for those with learning and literacy difficulties as these may be linked with the behaviour problem. PSPs can be used in primary and secondary phases and Circular 10/99 explains their development in more detail (pp.27-30).

Attention Deficit/Hyperactivity Disorder (AD/HD)

The classroom behaviour of children with AD/HD is often marked by a mixture of behaviours; typically, continually calling out, having short attention span, not following instructions and being oppressive to classmates.

However, all these behaviours are also typical of children with other problems such as language and communication difficulties or EBD. It is therefore important to remember that AD/HD is a medical definition which can only be diagnosed by doctors. Children diagnosed as having AD/HD are usually given the medication Ritalin. This is to help the child to concentrate and be able to take advantage of learning opportunities in school, and to lead a more normal life. The effective assessment and management of the child in the learning environment will be the teacher's responsibility. A structured and well-organised classroom environment, clear rules for behaviour and well-differentiated tasks will help such children learn.

Sensory and physical disabilities

Pupils with sensory difficulties such as hearing and vision, or motor impairment are likely to have been identified pre-school, or at least in the early years of schooling. For these pupils, access to the curriculum may be ensured through technical aids and equipment. Some will have individual programmes designed by specialist teachers or therapists. These may need to be carried out in school time.

Physical and medical difficulties

This term covers a number of more commonly found disabilities such as cerebral palsy which can affect the mobility and use of arms and hands and in some cases impairs speech. Other fairly common disabilities are spina bifida which can paralyse the lower body and impair perception, and muscular dystrophy where muscle tone weakens over time. There are also a number of rarer conditions which may affect the normal development of the body. Some of these require periods of treatment in hospital and extended therapy while attending school. (For further details see Kenward (1996) in Further Reading).

Health professionals will have assessed the needs of those with physical disabilities and their advice will have informed schools of extra equipment or therapies required. ICT is likely to be useful to help such pupils access the curriculum. Pickles (1998) states that:

'Teachers face a challenge to include children with physical difficulties in PE, dance and games lessons and to give them a range of activities which stretch them, but where they can achieve success.'

Therapists can give advice as to how this can be done.

Visual impairment (VI)

Those with severe impairment will have been diagnosed pre-school and many will have a Statement. Such children will be visited by peripatetic teachers who are trained in VI and will give advice on strategies and resources to support the child. There are some conditions, however, that occur as a result of accident or illness or that deteriorate over time. It is important, therefore, for all teachers to be vigilant and observant of signs of poor vision and eye strain. If in doubt ask for help through your SENCO or discuss the possibility of an eye test. As Miller (1996) reminds us, 'Healthy eyes are necessary for children to access everyday learning material, but eyes also give an indication of the general well-being of the child. Even minor visual problems can compound other learning difficulties'.

Hearing impairment

Conductive hearing loss is common, particularly in early childhood. It arises through infection of the middle ear and is often known as 'glue ear'. Children can have intermittent hearing loss which can go undetected. This can impair language development and make the learning of literacy skills more problematic. Conductive hearing loss is treatable once diagnosed.

Sensory-neural deafness is permanent impairment caused by damage to the nerves. It is more severe. It can be hereditary, but can also occur as a result of damage to the developing foetus or as a result of illness. Those with sensory-neural hearing loss may find some sounds more difficult to hear than others. Sounds may be distorted. Such losses are not amenable to medical treatment although hearing aids may make speech more accessible.

Hearing aids

Personal hearing aids are worn either behind or in the ear. They include a microphone to amplify sound, powered by batteries. The problem is that all sounds are amplified, so that the wearing of aids can be uncomfortable in certain situations. Hearing aid users only benefit in quieter classrooms. Children with partial hearing loss often rely on lip reading to enhance their learning. Teachers must therefore remember not to stand with their back to the light as this prevents lip reading.

Radio hearing aids
These allow children to accommodate more of the background noise and to be in direct touch with the teacher's voice. The child wears a radio receiver either plugged into the hearing aid or using a magnetic loop system. The teacher wears a small transmitter positioned so that the microphone is about 15cm from the mouth. Radio aids work when the teacher is the speaker but do not allow the hearing impaired child to hear other voices in the room. These aids are also bulky so some pupils particularly in adolescence find them embarrassing to wear. (Further information available on all of the above from NASEN Spotlights and INPUT series. See source lists.)

Inclusive practice

It is likely that a small proportion of pupils at the more severe end of the continuum will continue to need the specialised resources available in special schools. Parents often want special schools for such children. However, it is still possible to include pupils who attend special schools at sometime in mainstream programmes and activities. Such partnerships are encouraged in the Programme for Action (1998a).

The Programme for Action is encouraging schools to become more inclusive of those with SEN. This can mean working in partnership with a nearby special school so that pupils can attend mainstream classes on a part-time basis. It might mean staff of special schools working in the mainstream to support a pupil with SEN. Some LEAs have closed nearly all their special schools and therefore the large majority of pupils with Statements are in the mainstream schools with support from Learning Support Assistants (LSAs) and visiting specialist staff (see Chapter 9).

Chapter 3
The IEP within curriculum planning and differentiation

The previous chapter described the requirement for all teachers to identify and assess the needs of pupils that they teach. The original Code of Practice made a huge impact on the way schools recorded those with SEN and kept paperwork for pupils whose difficulties were seen to be significant enough to require IEPs. The Individual Education Plan has become established as a pivotal part of this procedure. Much of this has increased the paperwork for teachers and SENCOs alike. The procedures are seen as being necessary as a means of keeping track of those with SEN, for schools, LEAs, and for parents and pupils.

The influence of the Code of Practice (1994)

The status of the Code is unusual. It lies between a regulation and a circular in that it states that 'governors and schools should have regard to the Code of Practice'. In reality many schools and LEAs have behaved as though the Code were statutory. The effect of this has been to emphasise the accountability aspect of the special educational needs register and IEPs as opposed to more educational effects of curriculum planning.

The intention of the Code of Practice (1994) guidance was to identify children with learning difficulties and thus help them make progress within the curriculum. But the effect has often been too great an emphasis on setting and meeting individual's targets, in isolation from the lesson plans for the class. There also has not been an equivalent emphasis on whole-school curriculum planning which takes account of the special educational needs of each school's population.

This is probably due to the Code of Practice (1994) being introduced at the same time as the Dearing Revision of the National Curriculum. LEAs in particular focused their in-service training on the Code of Practice implications, particularly the Individual Education Plan. So it would appear that the Code of Practice has changed the focus for teachers. The individual needs must be stated and targets set, to be reached within a specific stated time, resulting in less time being spent on effective lesson planning to reduce the barrier to learning for those with SEN.

Target setting

There are different types of target. Some are short term and 'SMART' (Specific, Manageable, Achievable, Relevant and Timed) with definite measurable outcomes. But other targets are experiential, longer term or without precise measurable outcomes. Some targets relate to skills, some to conceptual understanding, some to self-awareness and organisational skills. Others relate to increased self-confidence and self-esteem (see Appendix for examples of targets set for specific case studies).

Behavioural targets are typically set by teachers and imposed on pupils. There are other targets which children can choose for themselves with support. Achieving self-determined targets strengthens pupils' coping ability. The first sign of progress may be an increase in confidence and a willingness to take charge of their own learning. Some individual targets will be necessary as will group targets, but it is important to check that target setting is not narrowing the curriculum and limiting progress or demotivating pupils. Enthusiasm, praise and a supportive learning environment will help all pupils move forward.

The effectiveness of educational targets will rest on their design and selection, as well as a shared belief of those involved that the targets are realistic and worthwhile. There are various ways of conceptualising target setting. Some will have direct linkage to outcomes, some flexible outcomes, but others will have outcomes that are recognised once they occur but were not predicted, (Tod, Castle & Blamires, 1998).

The Code of Practice (1994) led inevitably to separate work for pupils with SEN on their targets. This was often carried out by using support staff or by the teacher working with the child or group for a short time each day. This could result in improved progress for the pupil on those priority areas chosen for their development. Frequently, such targets covered aspects of literacy such as word recognition, spelling and handwriting, or aspects of numbers such as number bonds or learning tables.

But, as Carpenter et al (1996) points out, the Code needs a context which should be the curriculum. Furthermore he argues that targets for IEPs need to be embedded in the regular cycle of classroom activity married together with the learning experience offered to the child through the curriculum. If the planning process does not take account of this, the teachers are likely to have to keep two types of records; the IEP and the normal curriculum records with no correlation between the two. Targets should be planned within the programmes of study, but personalised for the child. Other targets may need to be cross-curricular and address skill acquisition, social development and self-esteem.

It is not always very clear how teachers use IEP information to plan lessons including differentiation or modification of the curriculum delivery. If the information about individual pupils is to have any impact on the way

27

lessons are planned and delivered, it is probable that a different approach is needed. The questions that need to be asked are:

- What do I need to know about this pupil which will affect the way I teach the class?

And then,

- What barriers to learning does this subject or topic present to this individual learner or group of learners?
- How can I modify my teaching strategies to ensure that pupils are making progress and remaining confident?

This is best illustrated by looking at some examples of specific lessons planned with reference to case studies as given in the Appendix.

Including pupils with Statements

Pupils with Statements of special educational need have the same curricular entitlement as others. Most Statements start the provision section with a sentence of this kind: 'He/she should have access to a broad and balanced curriculum (including the National Curriculum) differentiated to meet his/her needs and supported by teachers with expertise in whatever type of special need has been described.'

What does this mean for the pupil, their teacher and for the SENCO? Just how realistic is it to offer the broad and balanced curriculum, including the National Curriculum, to every pupil? Very few LEAs write any form of disapplication into Statements, although head teachers may apply later to do so. Most schools therefore endeavour to give access for all pupils to the whole curriculum on offer.

O'Brien (1998) sees differentiation as a legal entitlement and therefore the professional responsibility of teachers to develop teaching styles and approaches that meet the range of complex learning styles they encounter in the classroom. These approaches should be recorded as part of IEPs for those children with Statements.

The National Curriculum entitlement

The National Curriculum was revised in 1994 and again in 2000, giving more flexibility in its delivery, and more time to be spent on the individual needs of pupils who work with support or have technological aids or, when necessary, work outside the National Curriculum Key Stage of their peer group.

Figure 2 – Lesson Planning Example Form

Lesson planning to incorporate individual needs

Lesson topic

Core objectives for whole class

How will learning outcomes be assessed?

Teaching strategies and methods

Use of support [if available]

Learning characteristics of pupils with SEN

Barriers to learning for those with SEN in this lesson

Modifications required to accommodate pupils with IEP targets*

* May be covered by teaching strategies and methods with no further modifications required.

Figure 3 – Lesson Planning Example Form Year 1

Lesson planning to incorporate individual needs

(Example using Case Studies 1 & 4 in Appendix)

Lesson topic
Physical Education - small apparatus.

Core objectives for whole class
Improve ability to throw and catch balls and hoops or use of large hoops.
Improve co-operation in pairs.

How will learning outcomes be assessed?
Observation.

Teaching strategies and methods
Whole class activities with demonstration occasionally.
Praise for individuals and pairs.
Clear instructions to class and groups.
Alternative resources - see below.

Use of support [if available]
None.
Occasional advice from Physiotherapist for Case Study 1.

Learning characteristics of pupils with SEN
Case study 1 - Distractible and poor co-ordination in gross and fine motor skills.
Unsteady on feet.

Case study 4 - Difficulty in following instructions.

Barriers to learning for those with SEN in this lesson
Poor co-ordination will make catching small balls difficult - hand-eye co-ordination poor.

Listening to instructions can be difficult.

Modifications required to accommodate pupils with IEP targets*
Use groups to support individual children - pairs chosen with care.

Use large or soft objects for catching, e.g. bean bags/lightweight blow-up balls - sometimes work from a seated position.

Praise for approximate successes [see Pickles (1998) pp.84-86].

* May be covered by teaching strategies and methods with no further modifications required.

Figure 4 – Lesson Planning Example Form Year 3

Lesson planning to incorporate individual needs

(Example using Case Studies 2 & 5 in Appendix)

Lesson topic
Writing a letter to a friend or relation about your holiday.

Core objectives for whole class
To cover the vocabulary and phrases used in letters, and the verb tenses and verb agreement - use of past tense.

How will learning outcomes be assessed?
The letter and how it is written and oral contributions to lesson.

Teaching strategies and methods
- To have 4 differentiated tasks with different formats providing varying degrees of support, one allowing close procedure responses.
- Talk through sequence of events with groups.
- Use of sequences of pictures to illustrate a story.
- Reference words available around the room.

Use of support [if available]
LSA available.

Learning characteristics of pupils with SEN
Case Study 2 - Short concentration span, easily distracted, poor short-term memory, difficulties in following and retaining instruction, problems with visual/touch perception. Poor language, concentration, lacking confidence.

Case Study 5 - Problems with fine motor control [handwriting].

Barriers to learning for those with SEN in this lesson
- Concepts of language - vocabulary and spelling limitations. Requirement to write the letter independently.
- Handwriting - hampers ideas.

Modifications required to accommodate pupils with IEP targets*
- Tasks broken down into small steps. Check each step is understood. Give praise for each bit of success.
- Minimum writing for target children - record story on tape or use computer.
- Group support from pairs/peers with differentiated work.

* May be covered by teaching strategies and methods with no further modifications required.

31

Figure 5 – Lesson Planning Example Form Year 5

Lesson planning to incorporate individual needs

(Example using Case Studies 3 & 6 in Appendix)

Lesson topic
Numeracy Hour - using and reading timetables.

Core objectives for whole class
Being able to find the start and end of a journey or a TV programme and being able to state the duration of the journey or programme.

How will learning outcomes be assessed?
Written exercises and oral discussion, observation of tasks.

Teaching strategies and methods
- Practise changing 12 hour to a 24 hour clock times.
- Practise showing different ways of writing 30 minutes/¹/₂ hour; 15 minutes/¹/₄ hour.
- Reference available for checking.
- Use of groups/pairs - role play: phoning for times of journeys.

Use of support [if available]
None available.

Learning characteristics of pupils with SEN
Case Study 3 - Short concentration span and poor listening skills, short-term memory, limited sight vocabulary and problems with reading at word level and understanding meanings. Spelling takes time as does joined up writing - progressing but slow. Can be poorly organised, low self-esteem, needs praise.

Case Study 6 - Difficulty with sequences of numbers and clock hands positions. Difficulties reading clock times beyond hour/¹/₂ hour.

Barriers to learning for those with SEN in this lesson
Reading 24 hour times and relating this to known time concepts.
Sequencing days and months.
Concepts of time insecure at start.
Reading clock faces [minutes].

Modifications required to accommodate pupils with IEP targets*
- Practise counting seconds/minutes. Use egg timers to get the feel of time length in an accurate manner.
- Practise time words and have days and months available for reference.
- Some worksheets using only hours and half hours.

* May be covered by teaching strategies and methods with no further modifications required.

32

Figure 6 – Lesson Planning Example Form Year 9

Lesson planning to incorporate individual needs

(Example using Case Studies 7 & 8 in Appendix)

Lesson topic
MFL - French - 'Chat Up Lines' Words to help us talk to others in French.

Core objectives for whole class
- Being able to introduce yourself to others in French.
- Being able to find out information about others using key French phrases.
- Being able to let friends know where you live, likes and dislikes.
- To learn and reinforce the verbs avoir 'to have' and être 'to be'.

How will learning outcomes be assessed?
- Observation of role plays and interactions.
- Use of matching and sentence writing activities.

Teaching strategies and methods
- Watching and listening to video and audio tape role plays in target language using the key phrases.
- Being able to see, hear key phrases and sentences and read key phrases simultaneously from white board (using auditory and visual channels).
- Whole class response to phrases made by teacher.
- Small group role plays using question and answer cue cards with pictures and English translations
  - e.g. - Question: Quel age as tu? - Answer: J'ai quatorze ans.
- Matching word and short sentence picture cues and saying them in small group.
- Students to collect phrases and sentences they feel fairly confident with to write short introduction for their partner.
- Each partner to read to the other and each to translate.
- Students to make own memory cards to carry with them (they build up packs of different phrases and topics).

Use of support [if available]
- LSA working with smaller groups.
- French Assistant working with smaller groups.

Learning characteristics of pupils with SEN
Case Study 7 - Weak auditory short-term memory - weak auditory sequential memory and weak working memory; stronger visual memory, reluctant to join in oral work in whole class situations, reading age below chronological age. Oral work and oral language work much stronger than written work. Suffers from low self-esteem, in addition limited writing skills and poor organisation.

Case Study 8 - Visual presentation and cues. See teacher for lip reading.

Barriers to learning for those with SEN in this lesson
- Confidence to make attempts for fear of failure.
- Poor auditory processing for new sounds and phrases.
- Poor sequential processing for order of phrases at sentence level.
- Short concentration span.
- Impaired hearing.

Modifications required to accommodate pupils with IEP targets*
- As teaching and learning strategies indicate above but with further opportunities to hear phrases and sentences repeated using CD ROM, support from other adults.
- Packs of pocket size memory cue cards to review and practise main lesson content.
- Use of a Dictaphone to replay phrases as spoken by teacher/French Assistant to reinforce auditory memory.
- Use of group work with extra adult.
- Pre-teach vocabulary and phrases.
- Group work - one speaker at a time.
- Opportunities to have access to audio visual pre-lesson.

* May be covered by teaching strategies and methods with no further modifications required.

33

The term 'special educational needs' describes a continuum of need. Many pupils' identified needs are held in common with others in their class. Other, more exceptional, needs can be met with some additional support, resource or specialised form of teaching, which help access to the curriculum. A smaller group of children remain who may require smaller steps within the levels of the National Curriculum or further modifications to what is normally available.

It was thought that with the more flexible orders of the National Curriculum, following the Dearing Revision of 1994, it would be possible to make arrangements to vary curriculum assessment and delivery within the guidelines provided. The Access Statement (SCAA, 1996) gave permission for pupils to work outside the Key Stage of their class where necessary, but on material appropriate to their age. This means pupils can be assessed against the level descriptions given for each subject, and if necessary have a modified curriculum, but within the normal classroom context.

The Access Statement

The programme of study for each Key Stage should be taught to the great majority of children in the Key Stage, in ways appropriate to their abilities.

For the small number of children who may need the provision, material may be selected from earlier or later Key Stages where this is necessary to enable individual children to progress and demonstrate achievement. Such material should be presented in contexts suitable to the pupil's age.

Appropriate provision should be made for children who need to use:

- means of communication other than speech, including computers, technological aids, signing, symbols or lip-reading;
- non-sighted methods of reading, such as Braille, or non-visual or non-aural ways of acquiring information;
- technological aids in practical and written work;
- aids or adapted equipment to allow access to practical activities within and beyond school.

Appropriate provision should be made for those children who need activities to be adapted in order to participate in physical education.

Judgements made in relation to the level descriptions or end of Key Stage descriptions should allow for the provision above, where appropriate.

(SCAA, 1996)

Just what does access to the curriculum mean? It could mean that:

- Pupils all follow the same subject and content material, but use different means of access, often technical in nature;

or that,

- Pupils are exposed to the same experiences of each subject area and participate as fully as they can;

or that,

- Over time, pupils cover essential aspects required by the National Curriculum but the balance is achieved by focusing on core concepts and skills, sometimes using a cross-curricular delivery;

or that,

- the pupils move through the curriculum at a slower pace than their peers, inevitably leading to only a partial coverage of all the content.

Does differentiation work and is it sufficient?

It rather depends what is meant by the term. This needs exploration. At a most minimal interpretation, differentiation has become making different sets of worksheets or materials for different groups of pupils. This type of differentiation is often explained as differentiation by outcome. The pupils take what they can from the lesson and produce different levels of work as a result.

It is clear that in the first case 'death by paper' and overuse of worksheets can result in pupils feeling alienated by what is offered. In the second case the results of differentiation by outcome can be disappointing. The majority of the class may do well enough, but able pupils may underachieve, and others may even fail to complete any satisfactory work.

Clearly, a more radical view of what is meant by differentiation is needed. Interpretations include differentiation by resource, by support and by organisation. Perhaps the term should be abandoned and 'responsive pedagogy' used in its place.

Daniels (1996) argues that learners have the right to a responsive pedagogy as part of inclusive practice. He explains that this will apply at two levels; the first directs teaching and learning, the second organisation and management. To become effective schools need to develop learning systems which are fully responsive to feedback; this means making use of records to plan work using assessment information.

As the National Curriculum is organised and assessed by subject, it covers skills and areas of knowledge related to these subjects. But the curriculum in schools is intended to be wider than the National Curriculum and to include emotional and social development and a range of competencies and opportunities not written into the subject orders.

Daniels goes on to explain how we may need a change of value systems and practices. The use of behaviourist instruction determines the developmental sequence, but may limit the scope of the pupil's learning. An alternative approach, Daniels suggests, follows Vygotsky's position which was that there is a complex relationship between teaching and development in which the teaching and learning process is based on dialogue.

The broad aims of education apply to all children, but equally we must recognise the rights of the individual. This means taking into account differences of learning style and understanding particular barriers which some pupils have to overcome. As Rose (1998) says, 'the effective curriculum will be one which not only allows for individual differences but which also enables each pupil to reach his or her potential through a process of co-operative learning, within a school which celebrates the whole range of its pupils needs' (p.29). The curriculum should not be viewed as an end in itself, but rather as a framework through which we provide for learning.

Many teachers still argue that it is the National Curriculum that puts the most constraint on them in being flexible enough to meet the full range of needs. Others point out that it is the National Curriculum assessment and, in particular, the uses made of summative assessment at the end of Key Stages that add most restraint. The use of National Curriculum and GCSE grades for league tables has meant that achievement for those with some special educational needs is not acknowledged.

It seems very important for teachers to be able to conceptualise the curriculum in a variety of ways. Pupils with a wide range of ability can experience subject material and learn from it in different ways. They will not, however, all reach the same measured learning outcomes. Setting individual targets and school and national targets are very separate concepts.

The National Literacy Strategy (DfEE, 1998)

This sets out in detail just how the content of the Literacy Hour should be covered. It is also prescriptive about the exact pedagogy to be used. The rationale for these approaches arose from a mixture of research findings and looking at practice in successful classroom teaching.

The Literacy Hour is intended to give a vehicle for quality teaching of literacy. There are high expectations of what pupils can achieve through this National Strategy. This is because of the daily input which allows for practice and reinforcement. The structure of the hour with its class teaching and differentiated group work should stimulate, motivate and support pupils with learning difficulties. But to make sure this works well, a team approach will be required. Those involved are likely to be the SENCO, support teachers and assistants or parent helpers.

The Literacy Hour is intended to increase pupils' participation in understanding both text and word levels. However, extra work may still be needed outside the Literacy Hour to ensure progress for some pupils where difficulties are more complex. There are additional literacy support materials which are used in certain schools. (For more information see Further Reading.)

The National Numeracy Strategy (DfEE, 1998)

This should be adaptable for most pupils with learning difficulties. Its structure provides routines and security and there are clear expectations given. The emphasis on oral work may suit many children as long as they are properly supported. However, thought will need to be given when planning the Numeracy Hour to the particular needs of those in the class. These may include children with reading difficulties who cannot access the meaning of written instructions in mathematics. Questions will need to be carefully targeted and time given for some children to organise their thoughts before answering. Some mathematical vocabulary will need further explanation. There will need to be planned support for part of the Numeracy Hour for some groups. Other differentiation may be carried out by designing suitable resources and equipment or use of computer programmes. (See Berger, Denise & Portman, 2000; El-Naggar, 1996.)

The Government intends extending these strategies to the secondary sector from 2001.

The Revised National Curriculum (2000)

The new National Curriculum was published at the end of 1999. The intention is that the need to disapply pupils from the National Curriculum should be kept to a minimum.

The rest of the document explains in more detail some ways these principles can be put into practice. This can be found in an eight-page appendix at the back of each of the Subject Orders (booklets which set out the Programmes of Study for each subject in the National Curriculum).

This section reminds us that schools have the responsibility of providing a broad and balanced curriculum for all pupils. The document sets out three principles underlying the more inclusive curriculum. These are:

- setting suitable learning challenges;
- responding to pupils' diverse learning needs;
- overcoming potential barriers to learning and assessment for individuals and groups of pupils (QCA, 1999).

The revised curriculum also gives particular flexibility at Key Stage 4 so students may attend school part-time and have work experience or alternative provision for the remaining time. It is important for students with special needs to leave school with qualifications and certificates that will help them get work. This means that the opportunities at Key Stage 4 must be relevant to the pupil's needs, but also be valued by others, parents, further education providers and employers.

Now that there is a reduction in the number of subjects that must be taken, schools may disapply two subjects from Design and Technology, modern language and science. The new personal and social health education programme (PHSE) may also drive schools to develop cross-curricular skills and vocational courses.

Ways to develop curriculum planning

Pupils with SEN, especially those whose needs are severe or complex, may have to be helped to learn skills which other children pick up incidentally or are taught at home. A place needs to be found in the curriculum for self-help skills, learning organisational or social skills. Such a 'special' curriculum may fit within the National Curriculum, or could be timetabled for other parts of the day.

Those with severe and complex needs should be given opportunities to experience the full range of the curriculum even if not able to move forward very fast when compared with the rest of the class or age group.

Some record will need to be made of levels of participation for such pupils who are unable to attain specific skills within the area of chosen activity. For example, it may be important for children with significant difficulties to be exposed to quality literature, even if they cannot read. The way the curriculum is delivered must take account of disabilities so that the pupils do not suffer loss of self-esteem. Their contributions must be valued by teachers and peer groups.

Involving the pupils in the curricular planning process

Pupils have a right to take part in planning their own learning. This does not only mean asking questions of pupils at their Annual Review or a review of their IEP. It means involving all pupils in the daily process. In a positive learning environment, the whole class can be given problems to solve about curricular access. Pupils often find solutions that the teacher had not thought possible.

Involving the parents in the curricular planning process

'Children's progress will be diminished if parents are not seen as partners in the educational process' (Code of Practice, 1994, 2.28).

'Parents hold key information and have a critical role to play in their children's education' (Revised Code, 2000, 2.1).

Parents are very aware that schools should remember individual needs when planning curriculum delivery. Parents of pupils with complex needs often have different priorities for their child. These concern personal, social and life skills. Parents can also problem solve and have particular roles to play as they see their child from a different perspective. Parents can remind teachers to think in a cross-curricular way so that the child is not totally overwhelmed or confused by different approaches to topics. Some pupils react badly to change and need preparation which parents can do if involved early enough. Parents know, for example, how long ordinary tasks like eating and dressing can take for some children with complex disabilities. They can remind staff that homework also takes longer than average. All of these types of information can be used when planning IEPs, but may have more general implications for school policies.

Towards an inclusive curriculum

Wragg, in his book 'The Cubic Curriculum' (1997), has a useful way of conceptualising a future curriculum. He starts with three propositions which are: that education must incorporate a vision of the future; that there are escalating demands on citizens; and that children's learning must be inspired by several influences. This takes him to his final proposition that 'it is essential to see the curriculum as much more than a collection of subjects and syllabuses' (p.2). This leads him to propose a curriculum with different dimensions, of which the subject dimension is one, cross-curricular issues the second, and teaching and learning styles the third.

The model has much to offer as a way of including developmental and whole-child aspects so necessary for special needs work. For example, he points out the connection between emotion and motivation to learn. Wragg says that emotional states are an important part of the curriculum for many reasons. It could even be argued that emotional development should be a subject on the curriculum or a cross-curricular issue, but he places it in the third dimension as an element of teaching and learning, because it is something everyone must understand.

He ends by reminding his readers that pupils are partners in the process of change and improvement. They need to know about how to think and learn so they can become autonomous learners with the ability to work and live in harmonious groups. His model is therefore, in principle, a good description of an inclusive curriculum.

Chapter 4
Secondary school perspectives: SEN co-ordination and teaching and learning strategies

Introduction

The secondary school environment is a complex one. Therefore when considering students' learning needs it is necessary to use an eclectic approach. There will be a range of support systems and strategies in use at various levels within the school organisation. It is important, therefore, to consider a student's learning difficulties within the context of a whole-school problem-solving culture and not as isolated individual pathologies. Gross (1993) has referred to 'enabling' or 'disabling' learning environments. The intelligent school culture will view students not as having personal deficits, but rather, consider the learner's needs holistically, so ensuring the social and environmental climate of the school and classroom is tuned in to providing support for the learner and their learning needs. Some students may exhibit persistent and significant weaknesses, but all students will have potential strengths on which teachers can build.

The role of the SENCO and the learning support team

It is usual in the secondary school for the SENCO to be responsible for the overall management of the special needs policy. Some schools have devised alternative systems with shared responsibility; the approach will vary from school to school. The SENCO will liaise with class teachers, parents, students and outside agencies. It is a demanding role and the SENCO may have additional support from a deputy SENCO or other members of the learning support team. It is usual for the SENCO to be a member of the senior management team. The SENCO may also be a mainstream class teacher with a substantial teaching commitment.

Learning support teams within secondary schools vary in size and approach. The team may consist of subject specialists, teachers with specialist SEN qualifications or experience in SEN, and Learning Support Assistants (LSAs). How support teachers are allocated to classes and year groups will also vary, but it is probable class teachers will have a support teacher working with them in at least some of their classes.

In certain cases the support teacher will be assisting a particular student but in others they may focus on a group of students within the class. The approach will vary according to each class's learning profile, the school's learning support policy, the learning needs of individual

41

students and the views of parents and their children. SEN co-ordination requires an immense amount of consultation, negotiation, adaptability and imagination. Subject teachers and form tutors play an essential part in the learning support process, and time agreed for mutual planning will pay dividends.

In some schools the SENCO or support teachers have taken on the role of a teaching and learning consultant and will therefore carry out a more generic role. The SENCO role may involve working closely in lesson planning and preparation while also providing in-service training and advice on inclusive practice.

Many schools allocate co-ordination of individual year groups to specific members of the learning support team and they will work closely with class teachers, heads of year, form tutors, heads of department and heads of faculty. The initial procedures to be followed if a child is experiencing difficulty, will depend on the policy and procedures of each school. Since the introduction of the Code of Practice, many schools have followed its procedures for identification and assessment. But others have developed their own management and administrative approaches and embedded the procedures within whole-school assessment practice. Some innovative approaches have been developed in response to the Code of Practice which aim to promote consistency without uniformity.

In many cases the pastoral and learning divide that can exist has been reduced. Heads of year, heads of faculty, form tutors and learning support teachers may be responsible for students identified for School Action and School Action Plus, while the SENCO may take responsibility primarily for requests for statutory assessment and for those with Statements. It is important for all teachers to have a clear understanding of the school's SEN policy along with the procedures that accompany it. School SEN systems generally need to be pragmatic and flexible while also transparent and consistent. Innovative schools ensure that there are not false administrative boundaries dividing learning and behavioural procedures for the identification and assessment of student needs.

The Teacher Training Agency (TTA) Standards for SENCOs (1998) suggest that SEN requires whole-school co-ordination and co-operation rather than the reliance upon one key individual or mechanism. It is important to realise that a mechanistic approach will usually be inappropriate. The identification, assessment and approach to SEN should be an integral part of the school assessment policy, whole-school improvement strategies and therefore the responsibility, to some degree or another, of all staff.

Supporting individual needs and differentiation

There will be students in every class who at some stage will require extra support. It is important that teachers are aware of these students and have information about their learning needs. Teachers will need to meet with the SENCO, the learning support teacher or the head of year. When considering the learning needs of students, it may be necessary to meet with their form tutor. Good practice usually involves a discussion of any learning needs with a focus on the Individual Education Plan and how it complements the overall curriculum entitlement of the child. Teachers will want to discuss the IEP or Individual Behaviour Plan (IBP), if used, and incorporate or modify targets, strategies and outcomes in regard to the subject area. The IEP/IBP and any other additional information teachers have on individual students should become an integral part of planning, assessment, and record keeping. OFSTED (1999) reminds us that the IEP is written to indicate the type of knowledge, skills or understanding that a student requires in addition to the needs of other students in the class.

The learning support teacher or team will usually provide class teachers with pen portraits of identified students in each class in addition to the IEP/IBP, while also providing frameworks for differentiating subject specialist work. Teachers will also need IEP information to inform their own planning. At regular intervals you will be asked for information on the progress of individual students. This assessment data will be used in a range of forums and review meetings. Students will also need to use the range of information available on individual students to inform differentiated planning.

To ensure student entitlement and participation the curriculum will need to be differentiated. It is helpful to consider differentiation as a process rather than an event (see Chapter 3). In the secondary school environment it can function on at least two levels. Differentiation will be observed at the systems level, through the way whole-school structures and policies are organised and also in the way the school ethos and culture anticipates and values diversity. This will include the way a school:

- groups students and sets up opportunities for modules on study or revision topics;
- establishes the provision of support groups and systems for literacy acceleration or enrichment programmes for able students;
- promotes agreed school values and messages communicated through assemblies and personal social and health education development.

43

Such activities will exhibit whether or not the culture promotes an inclusive or an exclusive system of differentiation. Secondly, differentiation can be observed functioning at the micro level, through the way teachers plan and organise teaching and learning in their classrooms.

Differentiation of assessment and teaching

Some students will need to be provided with tasks and experiences that are tightly structured, while others will make more progress when learning experiences and outcomes allow for greater independence and are more open-ended. It is important for teachers to have a solid information base on each student so their planning is established on a range of evidence, which has been observed and recorded using differentiated assessment methods. These will include allowing students to respond to tasks in a number of ways and on a range of occasions. Student responses to tasks may include oral work, group presentations, self-assessment and evaluations, visual representations, tape recording, and informal conversations as well as the more formal approaches to recording achievement, while also ensuring that writing is not always the main mode of student response. The class teacher will need to communicate clearly the assessment process as well as ensuring there are opportunities to record unexpected outcomes.

Divergent responses from students, as a consequence of assessment, can easily be ignored, misinterpreted or devalued by the teacher. A framework that involves recording observations that reveal a student's strengths, interesting points and areas for development (Strengths, Interesting observations, Development – SID) is a useful one. Such a system is not too administratively onerous, is practical to use within the busy classroom and provides an analytical tool which is evidence-based. The SID system allows the teacher to assess progress as well as areas for target setting in the future.

It may not be practicable or appropriate to match planning to the individual needs of all the students in a class. So although planning will go as far as it can to match students' needs, at times there will be a gap between intention and action. It is important to realise secondary age students are still developing new or different knowledge, understanding, skills and attitudes. These areas develop at a fast rate and the ebb and flow of the adolescent developmental process will certainly have an impact on the planning and dynamics of the classroom environment. It will therefore be necessary to develop a responsive approach to student needs, based on assessment and observation.

Multi-sensory approaches

All students in the mainstream classroom will learn more effectively if the teacher uses a multi-sensory approach. This involves using the auditory, visual and kinaesthetic/tactile (VAKT) senses as an essential part of the classroom learning experience. Some students will display strengths in particular channels or modalities and therefore it will be necessary to ensure teaching style is evaluated, so that teachers are aware of the modalities that they use predominantly. Teachers may not be able to always achieve a deep knowledge of all student strengths. However, by using the VAKT framework teachers will not be focusing exclusively on any one modality.

Students who exhibit auditory strengths usually remember what is said in class and may prefer class discussion; however, they may not be as good with written instructions. Students who exhibit visual strengths will usually remember information in picture form and perhaps be less able to concentrate or learn from discussion or classroom talk. Kinaesthetic learners tend to remember and associate with activities that allow them to move about and perhaps act out or present information in the form of a role play; they may recall action observed far more easily than if they just read or heard it. It is important to realise that no student will learn through just one modality as each channel or modality impacts with another. The poor auditory learner who is using a diagram or mind map to understand and remember a sequence of events in history or a mathematical formula should also be encouraged to sub-vocalise or read the information to themselves. The use of such a strategy will use the visual channel to reinforce the weaker auditory memory. In the same way, if students with poor visual and auditory channels are given the opportunity to watch other students presenting information through drama or role play, the kinaesthetic modality is activated, but the visual and auditory channels are also being reinforced.

Cognitive styles and teaching strategies

Vail (1992) suggests that some learners are 'pyramid builders' or 'parachute jumpers', while Chin (1992) has referred to 'grasshoppers' and 'inchworms'. Both these metaphors are simple but effective illustrations and aides-memoires for the busy classroom teacher. Students who are 'pyramid builders' will prefer to work and move forward in a sequential way, step by step; learning for the 'pyramid builder' or 'inchworm' needs to be linear, and well structured. Learners who are 'parachute jumpers' or 'grasshoppers' prefer to be introduced to the global concept, starting at the deep end, and will tend to see the whole picture. There are, however, no pure types of learner as good learners will use all modalities and styles. The teacher will want to encourage students by using a range of modalities and styles as an essential part of their classroom repertoire; in this way weaker learning modalities and styles will be supported by stronger ones.

It is sometimes the case that when teachers fail to acknowledge students' individual learning styles difficulties can emerge. Such difficulties may have more to do with the learning tasks, classroom experiences and a certain teaching style than they do with individual pupils' special educational needs.

Conceptualising intelligences

It will be helpful to teachers if they are aware of Gardner's (1993) criticisms of the traditional view of intelligence: he has provided an alternative concept for teachers to consider. Gardner's work suggests that teachers should not be asking how intelligent a student is, but instead asking what type of intelligence or intelligences does the student have? He has described seven types of intelligence:

- Linguistic – words and language.
- Logical – mathematical – numbers and reasoning.
- Spatial – pictures and images.
- Bodily – kinaesthetic – body and hands.
- Musical – rhythm and tone.
- Interpersonal – social understanding.
- Intrapersonal – reflection, insight and knowledge of self.

Gardner's model of intelligence provides a practical framework for inclusive practice. It allows the teacher to not only consider students as individuals with different abilities and diverse potential but can also be used in relation to teaching and learning styles, as a template for a more sophisticated approach to planning. Armstrong (1994) has used Gardner's list of intelligences to suggest a range of teaching activities.

Such a framework provides a useful teaching and learning device from which to monitor and evaluate the teaching and learning process. Planning teaching and learning using such a template can prevent SEN, and will ensure inclusion and effective learning for a wider range of students.

Classifying classroom tasks

Stevenson and Palmer (1994) have developed a useful classification for monitoring classroom tasks. They have suggested seven areas of classification which in addition to Gardner's model provides teachers with a framework for planning and monitoring the teaching and learning process. Their classifications are:

1. incremental – introduces new ideas, procedures or skills, demands recognition and discrimination;
2. restructuring – demands the invention or discovery of idea, process or pattern;
3. enrichment – demands application of familiar skills to new problems;
4. practice – demands the tuning of new skills to familiar problems;
5. revision – demands the use of knowledge and skills previously learnt and the bringing back of such material into the conscious state;
6. discovery – demands exploration of an open-ended nature with unpredictable outcomes;
7. problem-solving – demands an approach similar to discovery but the learner will usually have a clear understanding of the end product.

Stevenson and Palmer further suggest that while the seven classifications exist independently, they also interweave as a dynamic part of the teaching and learning process. The classifications, therefore, provide the teacher with an excellent aide-memoire or framework when planning for progression and diversity, both within subject areas and for cross-curricular understanding. Using the classifications to structure and audit planning will enable teachers to provide appropriately matched and challenging activities for most students, including those who are more or less able.

Planning for group work

Group work needs to be well planned in advance and it is advisable to vary the group compositions on a rolling programme. Group composition could include mixed ability, mixed gender, same gender, friendship pairings or by ability. As the teacher gets to know classes they may also wish to group students with reference to their cognitive styles. Planning for group work is generally not considered carefully enough by teachers, but its importance cannot be emphasised enough. Thoughtfully constructed groups also ensure that students are a learning resource for each other.

The link between teaching styles and behaviour management

There is an inextricable link in the relationship between classroom learning styles, student motivation and concentration, and student behaviour. A consideration of these areas along with the use of teaching and learning styles and the use of different modalities does not guarantee students' learning and behaviour will always be perfect. However, if consideration is given to students' underlying strengths and preferences, as well as their weaknesses, it does mean that in the main teachers will be constructing some of the essential curriculum-based frameworks for positive behaviour management.

Language and literacy support

The Government intends to extend the National Literacy Strategy into secondary schools. A number of schools already have in place literacy and language acceleration programmes in Key Stage 3. These may involve intense literacy sessions which revisit basic skills while also encouraging greater language awareness and experience across the curriculum. It is important that multi-sensory approaches are integrated into literacy or language programmes. The Basic Skills Agency (1997) have produced materials and guidance to encourage and support language and literacy in the curriculum and such an approach in collaboration with specialist programmes can do much to improve student achievement in the secondary school. Some schools have initiated projects that involve 'buddy' or peer mentoring systems where older or more skilled learners support younger or less able students with reading and spelling.

Language development

Sound language development and acquisition is a prerequisite for learning. Students with limited language experience or difficulties will be vulnerable in the mainstream curriculum and so clear strategies will be needed to ensure that they are not crushed by the demands of the curriculum. Such children may have limited vocabularies or difficulties with precise word meanings and they may be slow in the association of words with meanings they already know. They do not easily understand the multiple meanings in different contexts or shades of meaning and so comprehension can be limited. It is therefore important to provide students with language and structures that enable full inclusion. It is important to acknowledge that a pupil who has expressive language difficulties may need more time and possibly advance warning of opportunities to contribute to discussion.

Teachers will need to consider pupils' prior experiences, what they already know and what can be drawn on. Many pupils with difficulties in this area have developed a low self-esteem and are suffering from poor 'emotional literacy'.

Specific literacy difficulties

It is important for teachers to use the VAKT framework as a structure for planning and progression in this area. Information and new knowledge needs to be presented in a form that allows students to receive information in all modalities. Students may also need more time for written exercises or to be provided with structures to aid reading for meaning and comprehension such as Directed Activities Related to Texts (DARTs). Writing frames to support reports and essay writing and the organisation of ideas can also be helpful. Teachers should consider also the use of study skills training both implicitly as part of lesson delivery and also as explicit skills taught as a whole school or department programme. If schemes of work are planned on a modular basis it should be manageable to include study skills or learning about learning sessions as part of the department programme.

Strategies to support students who experience language and literacy difficulties
Aim to:

- provide key technical and specialist vocabulary by lesson, module, and term;
- introduce new or technical vocabulary at the start of the lesson or topic;
- display key language on walls and displays e.g. keep and illustrate a vocabulary list;
- provide key vocabulary for study skills such as investigate, evaluate, summarise, observe, compare, contrast, present, describe, discuss. Does the language of the question allow the pupil to access the task?
- teach the use of concept or word maps to show linguistic and semantic connections between words;
- use games to revisit language and to practise, rehearse and reinforce learning until automatic.

While teaching:

- keep instructions short and concise;
- make eye contact and moderate exposition making sure you summarise and provide information in a visual form;
- be aware of how you or texts use abstract language, metaphor and figures of speech;
- establish a way to communicate with students so that when they do not understand they can let you know without attracting the attention of their peers;
- encourage students to repeat questions or instructions to themselves – sub-vocalisation;
- let students use tape recorders, Dictaphones or work with a mentor;
- do not provide key information or tasks at the end of the lesson;
- let students and their parents know that you are aware of their SEN – this can prevent anxiety and limit frustration and poor communication.

At the secondary phase students experiencing language and literacy difficulties will need support and intervention on a number of fronts, including the development of greater self-esteem through the enhancement of skills, but also as part of a programme which demystifies the learning process. This should occur as part of the mainstream subject curriculum as well as being established through other support programmes. Some schools will identify students to attend support groups in relation to behaviour management, low self-esteem or learning needs.

Learning to learn

For some secondary age students learning is still a mystery they have not yet managed to acquire and they may have decided it is not worth the bother. They may also have come to view themselves as limited with no potential for achievement or academic success.

There are no panaceas with which to transform students who have acquired such experiences and attitudes. However, if planning is part of a reflective process it is possible to motivate students who are stuck and help them progress. It is also important to communicate implicitly and explicitly that learning is not a gift but a skill that can be learnt. Students' attitudes and views on learning can be improved when they realise they do have the potential to achieve academically and taste success. Teachers often feel there is not sufficient time to address learning skills; however, if students do not have an awareness of how to learn, relatively straightforward and low level learning needs can easily become deep-seated special needs.

Some of the key elements of demystification and meta-learning should include:

- providing students with opportunities to evaluate and reflect on how they learn;
- teaching strategies for time management and the organisation of work;
- opportunities to engage in problem-solving and thinking skills including use of concept mapping;
- giving outlines and templates for key research strategies for the organisation of thinking;
- frameworks for the organisation of thinking, writing and reports;
- use of ICT for disaffected writers and students with poor motor skills.

Cross-curricular approaches to knowledge, skills and understanding

For many students in the secondary school, learning is perceived to be all about unrelated subjects and dislocated facts. Students can often perceive a lack of cohesion between curriculum subjects and areas of knowledge, and even able students can fail to see important connections that may exist.

Curriculum guidance from a range of sources has indicated the benefits of linking related knowledge and skills across subject areas. Effective learning takes place when students are able to make links with previous knowledge, skills and experiences. Students who experience difficulties with learning need plenty of opportunities to practise and over-learn new ideas while also being encouraged by their own progress and maintaining concentration and motivation. Making links with other curriculum areas will allow students to revisit knowledge, concepts and skills leading to scaffolding, reinforcing, and consolidating language and learning.

Schools will organise cross-curricular links in a range of different ways, both formally and informally. For example, students working on an art portfolio can draw upon work covered in English, drama or science, or vice versa. Such an approach allows for the different stages of interaction within the curriculum context as well as supporting and encouraging literacy and language development beyond the range of individual subjects. A cross-curricular approach also ensures the classification of tasks takes place across the curriculum and not just within subject departments.

A cross-curricular approach will also ensure that planning for the needs of students with SEN will include targets in IEPs which embrace a range of learning outcomes. In using cross-curricular strategies the process of transferring information from weaker short-term working memory, visual or auditory memory, to long-term memory is optimised and therefore there is a greater chance of consolidation and successful understanding.

Teachers having regard to a cross-curricular approach, which is also set within the context of learning to learn, will be planning to support the learning needs of all students including those with SEN.

Supporting diverse learning needs at Key Stage 4

The Revised National Curriculum (2000) maintains the theme of entitlement and participation for all students. Students working at Key Stage 4 have been given greater flexibility and choice. It is necessary for teachers at Key Stage 4 to provide challenge and expectation while also ensuring that the drive for results does not diminish the need for continued educational care. Planning for student diversity at Key Stage 4 will build on the range of approaches to teaching and learning used during previous Key Stages, but in addition will need to include:

- early counselling and target setting in partnership with both students and parents about programmes of study choices. This should be based on a range of evidence including baseline scores, SATs and teacher observations;
- considered and mutual decisions about appropriate modification of some programmes of study as is possible in Design and Technology, modern foreign languages and science, so as to allow students greater opportunities for concentration and reinforcement in chosen areas;
- provision of assessment information on students who may be entitled to examination concessions, such as, additional time, use of information and communications technology and a reader or an amanuensis;
- careful planning and discussion of students' work-experience placements so as to ensure inclusion of their personal needs, interests and strengths which will have a direct influence on students' confidence and self-esteem;

- the consolidation of cross-curricular links through key skills as described in the new National Curriculum;
- public accreditation which is realistic and flexible and may include combined programmes of GCSE, GNVQs, Award Scheme Development Accreditation Network (ASDAN) and other accredited pathways;
- internal school accreditation through Records of Achievement, internal certification and the recognition and celebration of achievement;
- option support sessions which allow students to review and reinforce programmes of study; receive individual and small group support for coursework and general organisation; revision of basic skills, study skills and thinking skills;
- opportunities to link review sessions directly with realistic personal targets and expectations for further accreditation or careers experience.

The new National Curriculum has set out a useful statement of values as well as the statutory duty for schools to provide students with teaching in citizenship education. The aim must be, for both the values underpinning teaching and learning at Key Stage 4 and the tightly defined 'learning outcomes' which define citizenship, to ensure school communities work as close knit teams in order to support student diversity and promote social justice.

Where the whole school and class teacher are continually working to create and maintain an enabling environment, the learning needs of most students will be provided for. If such an enabling environment has been established as an essential part of a school's problem-solving culture, only a smaller group of students will still experience persistent difficulties. It is these students who will be identified as requiring additional or special educational support through IEPs, outside agencies and possibly Statements of SEN.

Chapter 5
Working with Learning Support Assistants:
A team approach

In recent years there has been a growth in the employment of Learning Support Assistants (LSAs) or Teaching Assistants (TAs), the names used by the DfEE, to support children with special educational needs, usually for those with a Statement. Some primary schools also employ their own LSAs to work with groups of pupils on earlier stages of the Code of Practice. It is therefore important that all teachers learn how to work with LSAs and develop a team approach to supporting pupils with a range of SEN.

In primary schools, the partnership of LSA and class teacher can be most effective, if given enough liaison and planning time. It is the role of head teachers and SENCOs to support the development of this teamwork by allocating some 'official' time for planning. LSAs also need to be given opportunities for training. Without the recognition that time has to be allocated, this most valuable extra support resource can be wasted.

The role of the LSA in the secondary school is a developing one. LSAs make a major contribution to the progress of the students they support and are an important facilitator of inclusive classroom practice. The LSA's actual role will vary according to the range of children with SEN and the way the learning support process is managed within the school. In most cases the LSA will be supporting children in the classroom.

LSAs may perform a particularly important role in supporting children with physical or sensory impairments working in practical subjects such as science or technology. They may also be involved in developing resources and differentiating work. The LSA can bring a wide range of knowledge, skills and experiences to the school.

LSA roles and responsibilities

An effective LSA will be flexible and may from time to time carry out many tasks. However, it is important that she/he has a clear job description provided by the school, some induction into her/his job, probably provided by the SENCO, and opportunities to review her/his work in a professional way with someone on the staff. Where there are several LSAs in a school, regular meetings often take place with the SENCO for reviewing practice and offering some 'on the job' training. LSAs should not be left in charge of the whole class and if working with a group this should take place in the classroom, or in a part of the school where other staff are available if necessary.

As the SENCO's role develops and involves them in a wider range of management and administrative responsibilities and LSA professional training is extended, the LSA's role in monitoring individual students' IEPs and record keeping will also be enhanced.

LSAs are invaluable for monitoring activities such as the use of computers and supervising classroom games designed for specific purposes. LSAs can be asked to prepare specific materials or equipment needed for a child or a group with SEN. This might mean enlarging work for a visually impaired pupil, preparing audio tapes and helping record information on a Dictaphone.

All LSAs may require help with the details of record keeping, for example on keeping a diary. They will also need advice as to how best to communicate with parents and issues of confidentiality.

Working on IEP targets

Pupils with or without Statements will have IEPs which set targets. Part of the strategy to meet these targets may be to offer additional support from an adult, a teacher, LSA or occasionally a volunteer parent. This adult works alongside the child in class. Their role is to help the pupil be as independent a learner as possible. So the adult will check that instructions have been understood, keep the pupil on task by encouragement and praise, as well as add additional teaching points. This type of support is often given by LSAs and is particularly productive for younger pupils.

A well-planned small-step approach to a piece of learning may be one strategy employed as part of an IEP. This type of work sets very small achievable targets which can be measured easily. The purpose is to help the child achieve success, albeit over a very small piece of learning.

If a teacher explains such a small-step programme, then the LSA can work on these targets with the pupils for just a few minutes daily. It might be learning a practical skill, such as dressing or self-care with a young child, or it might be a programme to reinforce aspects of learning, e.g. number bonds or handwriting.

Other types of target may be set which apply across the day and are more concerned with organisational skills or with behaviour. Again, LSAs can help the child understand the target and record and reward them when they achieve it.

Adult support is most often given to small groups, even when the target child is the one for whom it was allocated. Pupils need time and space to attempt tasks, make and learn from mistakes and develop autonomy. An over-protective type of support will suppress independence.

However, whatever individual support is available, it cannot compensate for a poorly differentiated curriculum. If the focus is solely on the child and not the curriculum and classroom content, this form of support may fail. This is, of course, one of the dilemmas of SEN; the tension between meeting individual needs and the requirements of accessing the core National Curriculum.

There are different ways to conceptualise how support is given. You can see support as being given direct to a single child or student who has a Statement, but another way of working is to build teams of adults who together support the teaching and learning process through the delivery of the curriculum.

Support for the curriculum

This view of support can be seen as an additional means of ensuring that the curriculum is accessible to a wider range of pupils. It often takes the form of collaborative partnerships where both adults plan and deliver aspects of the subject and where good use of group work is possible.

For many teachers, having another adult in their classroom presents a threat to their control or a fear of criticism of their work. Even when both adults are happy to work together there are difficulties to overcome. There needs to be a flexible approach to support both the curriculum, the teacher and the child or group of children. Ground rules about control, and beginnings and ends of lessons need to be established.

There are no set rules; each pair or team needs to work out what is best for their own context. The best partnerships recognise the different strengths of its members, allow control of content, delivery and assessment to be shared. A typical team is a class teacher and one LSA. Tasks such as whole-class teaching are the teacher's responsibility, as is the planning of the lesson. LSAs, on the other hand, are very good at understanding children's emotional and social needs, preparing materials under guidance and carrying out well-planned IEPs, if the strategies and targets have been explained.

LSAs can support the curriculum too, not by planning whole lessons, but by sharing ideas of how to follow up a theme or produce a resource. LSAs often say, during training sessions, that they are an underused resource: 'If teachers would only explain what they want the children to do – we could prepare better and get materials together.'

Building support teams

LSAs often have to work with other professionals over specific programmes for Statemented pupils. For certain children whose needs are complex and who may have a Statement covering a mixture of difficulties, it will be necessary to build up a support team. The members of this team will vary but are likely to include the class teacher, SENCO, the LSA and the parent, as well as any visitors from the network of health and educational professionals who give advice about programmes for the child.

Children with physical difficulties or language and communication problems often have programmes devised by a physiotherapist or a speech and language therapist. Such programmes often require some daily practice or exercises. If these are explained to LSAs they can help this regular practice take place and record progress. Such a team will need to communicate easily so that there is no confusion for the child, the parent or indeed for the class teacher.

It is important that the professional who devised the programme returns on a frequent basis to check that it is being delivered correctly. They should observe the LSA with the child if at all possible to ensure everything is being carried out correctly.

Planning before the child arrives at the school

If a youngster with complex needs is due to arrive at your school, advanced planning must take place. Questions will need to be answered about access to the building, mobility within the school and access to the curriculum through technical aids such as computers. An LSA may need to be hired by the school and given an induction programme so that he/she learns about the child and their disabilities.

The LSA needs to understand their role in supporting pupils with physical disabilities or health problems and how they will work with the support team. For example:

- Will they be required to work under the direction of a therapist to carry out specialist programmes?
- Will they need to be trained to use specialist equipment such as computers or communication aids?
- Will they need to help toilet pupils and deal with personal hygiene for those with physical disabilities?

(for more information see Further Reading)

Support for pupils with emotional or behavioural difficulties

'Emotional and/or behavioural difficulties (EBD)' is a term used to cover a wider range of conditions. However, usually children are troubled themselves or cause trouble to others. They may have social problems ranging from shyness, anxiety and compulsions to those who 'act out' or are aggressive.

This group of pupils presents a different kind of challenge when planning support. Clearly they too need access to the curriculum and help to overcome blocks to learning which arise from their internal state of anxiety or fear of risk taking. Teachers too need a different quality of support when facing challenging or worrying behaviour, establishing classroom rules and building positive relationships. For pupils with challenging behaviour, LSAs will need some understanding of behaviour management techniques and classroom rules.

LSAs are often employed to work alongside a pupil with a Statement for EBD. It is important that they understand the learning needs this child may have as well as helping them to conform to reasonably acceptable behaviour. A typical feature of children with emotional difficulties is that they are very afraid of failure. A key role of the LSA will be to encourage the child to 'have a go' and to praise his/her efforts. Keeping careful records will also mean the child can see his/her success.

LSAs should receive some training from either the school's SENCO or LEA advisory and support staff. Professionals from these services should be able to advise on the best strategies to manage pupils with emotional and behavioural difficulties.

Fox (1998) lists key ways of helping those with EBD. She suggests:

- Take every opportunity to improve self-esteem of the pupil.
- Give appropriate rewards or praise.
- Develop LSA's own listening skills.
- Encourage pupil to take responsibility.
- Point out good role models.
- Try to anticipate trouble.
- Deal with behaviour in a positive way.
- Be realistic in what can be achieved. (p.62)

Developing flexible working practices

Where a school employs several LSAs, a flexible way of managing the team will help pupils not to become too dependent on one adult. When illness strikes, such an approach can prepare pupils for changes, so they are not too dependent on one adult. However, each child needs their key worker, who will work with them for the majority of the time. Any changes of this sort will need to be explained to parents.

Liaison time

Successful collaborative partnerships are made, not born, and are a product of continual careful negotiation. The classroom context is part of the experience that affects children's individual responses to learning. Working together, adults can help each other make sense of the complexity of the classroom environment. Successful teams will use time to analyse the various elements of classroom interactions and evaluate how support can best contribute to solving the various problems that arise. The problem is that time is scarce and rarely of sufficient quality to allow this to happen. Liaison time is often not seen as a priority by senior management, but without liaison time, what could be the most effective way to support the curriculum and the child with SEN can be ineffective and this considerable additional resource could thus be wasted.

When these teams are working effectively, it is often possible to split classes into groups where the teacher moves between groups and the LSA stays with her own group, but may keep an eye on another one nearby. LSAs develop their own perspective of the classroom, its management and dynamics and can often offer ideas to the teacher from their observations.

Communication in secondary schools

In secondary schools it is particularly important to ensure that time is given to communicating both your immediate lesson aims and objectives as well as your medium-term planning with the LSA; team planning will provide the most effective teaching and learning environment. Whether it is planning with the LSA or other adults, such as a language support teacher, it is always important to confirm and clarify roles. Finding time for such planning is not always easy, but even planning sessions organised regularly, rather than longer meetings arranged less frequently, can enhance the classroom environment for all.

The secondary school environment is both complex and busy, therefore good communication systems are essential. LSAs may act as intermediaries between family and pupils, and teachers; they can be the 'eyes and ears' of the teacher. Establishing clear roles and responsibilities with and for the LSA is necessary in order to ensure an effective approach to inclusive classroom practice.

Support for the teacher

This may not seem very different from the support for the curriculum, but perhaps is more to do with partnering, of a different kind. It occurs most when LSAs or parents work for large parts of the day in one class or where support is otherwise available on a regular basis. Support is then seen as a resource which the teacher manages along with organisation of tasks and the physical resources of materials and space. From this point of view, the teacher is the room manager in charge of the team and as part of this managerial role, deploys the time of extra adults to particular tasks. The teacher is supported if this room management is efficient and everyone knows their role.

The opportunities that are presented by routine working partnerships are tremendous. Better differentiation and group work can take place. Learning can better be mediated by an adult working with the pupils to enhance thinking and language.

Room management: an example of planning classroom support

At its best, the classroom team with an LSA and teacher working together can bring about very effective learning for pupils with SEN and others in the class. What makes such teams effective is explored by Thomas (1992) who carried out research into both the planning and practice aspects of this partnership. He suggests that it is not best practice to leave team-building to chance by relying on good relationships worked out over time. From his research there is evidence that some agreement is needed about the potential roles of all those in a classroom at any one time. He calls such planned organisation of roles 'room management' and takes some of the ideas from excellent work done in special schools. The tension for a class teacher is to manage both the individual needs of pupils and the activity of the whole class. Splitting these roles, for any one period of time, and giving the role of 'individual helper' to one adult and 'activity manager' to the other, increases on-task behaviour of pupils. These roles can be reversed at certain times, but the change round should also be part of the planning. If more than two adults are available, then they too can be assigned as second 'activity 'or 'individual helpers' or be the 'mover'. This last role is to keep the flow of the activity going by doing the housekeeping tasks of fetching equipment, sharpening pencils etc.

Some ways to get started with a new LSA

- Introduce the LSA to the class. Make sure the children know you respect the LSA as someone who will be helping the class.
- Give the LSA some ideas of your classroom rules and make it clear how far you see it as her/his role in helping you with the management of the class.
- Give the LSA information (from the Statement, for example) about their child and others they will work with on a regular basis, but remind them of confidentiality of such information.

- Help organise the LSA's time, especially in the first weeks.
- Suggest how you would like the LSA to keep records of the work done with the target individual.

Some golden rules for LSAs

They should always try to 'do themselves out of a job' by helping the child become more independent of them. Being over-protective is not helpful when building up confidence, autonomy and self-esteem. However, 'being there' at the right time is also an art a good LSA develops. It may be to head off an argument, mediate a situation, give a little encouragement or praise. It may be that specific help is needed in reading or interpreting instructions or helping the child check his/her work.

Chapter 6
Getting some further help from the
multi-professional networks

Rights to services

For those children who have more complex needs, teachers may well need advice from other professionals who may come from the education services or from the health services or, occasionally, from social services. It is usually the SENCO or head teacher who makes the referral to outside agencies or services. They must inform the parent first and explain why such a referral is seen as helpful. In most cases the parent must give their permission if the child is to be assessed individually. Sometimes, however, advice can be sought for teachers to help in the management of groups of pupils.

The Revised Code advises that schools should always consult specialists when they take action on behalf of a child through School Action Plus. But involvement of specialists can play an important part in the very early identification of SEN (Revised Code, para. 10.1).

'Special educational needs support services can play an important part in helping schools identify, assess and make provision for children with special educational needs. Such services include specialist teachers of children with hearing, visual, and speech and language impairments, teachers in more general learning and behavioural support services, educational psychologists and advisors or teachers with a knowledge of information technology for children with special educational needs.'

(Code of Practice, para. 2:58)

'Schools should work in close partnership with the providers of all these services. The SENCO in particular should be aware of the LEA's policy for provision of support services and how the school can gain access to them.'

(Revised Code, Chapter 10.1)

Educational services

The SENCO is the most likely person in your school to make the referral, so if you feel you need extra advice from a specialist, it is to the

SENCO to whom you should first make the request. The SENCO should have an idea of who is available to help and be able to advise on the best procedures for doing so. This should all be made clear in your SEN policy.

There are certain services to be found in all LEAs while others are only sometimes available. Each LEA must have educational psychologists and education welfare officers who work for the LEA. These services are mandatory. Other support services are usually available from the education authority, although in some areas, where funds have been delegated to schools, these services, if still present, are made available through a service level agreement.

The LEA has a duty under the Code of Practice to inform schools of education services that are available and how these should be accessed and funded. LEAs must ascertain the demand for the SEN services from schools (DfE, 1994b).

Schools and their governors have responsibilities under the Code to identify, assess and make provision. Maintained schools must publish information that includes the school's arrangements for working in partnership with LEA support services, health and social services and the 'Connexions' service (Code of Practice, 2000, para. 10.1).

Schools Psychological Services

Each LEA has a Schools Psychological Service. It will be headed by a Principal Educational Psychologist and consist of a team of educational psychologists (EPs). Together they cover all nursery, primary, secondary and special schools in the LEA. They are also available to parents and children in the pre-school stage usually from the age of 2. The service also gives advice to the LEA itself.

EPs have a statutory duty to carry out assessments of those pupils who have been put forward for statutory assessment under the Code of Practice Assessment. EPs must carry this out within the timescale laid down by the Code. EPs usually see the pupil in school, talk to the teachers and parents and possibly liaise with other professionals. They then write a report of the assessment which becomes an Advice. This helps the decision making process about whether a Statement is required. If a Statement is drafted it becomes one of the Appendices to that Statement.

EPs also try to be available to their schools for more general advice on request from the school SENCO or head. Many EPs allocate individual schools a proportion of their time to be used as the school chooses.

Education Welfare Officers (sometimes called Education Social Workers)
Education Welfare Officers (EWOs) are employed by the LEA to help parents and the LEA meet statutory obligations in relation to school attendance. They can play an important role with pupils who also have SEN, in helping liaise between home and school and keeping communication going in cases where attendance is sporadic. There are often underlying reasons for poor attendance which relate to learning or behavioural difficulties. Partnership between SENCOs and EWOs can be very productive in sorting out some of these underlying difficulties and easing a pupil back into school.

Special Needs Education Officers
Each LEA will have a Special Needs Education Officer who has the responsibility for the Statementing procedure. They are likely to have a team of people working for them to carry out all the paperwork and to liaise with schools, parents and professionals. Sometimes this service is arranged on a casework basis where each officer is responsible for a group of cases from the first referral through to the draft Statement and beyond into monitoring the Annual Review process. The Special Needs Education Officer will have decision making powers sometimes working with a panel or representative, with schools and other professionals. This panel will decide on the evidence from schools or parents and decide which pupils go forward for a multi-professional assessment. When all the advice from these assessments are gathered, the panel will also decide which cases will go forward to the draft Statement.

Teachers, other than SENCOs, are unlikely to have much direct contact with this department. However, the decisions made will often affect the classroom teacher who may be waiting to hear if a child will get a Statement and what provision will be granted.

Learning Support Services
These now vary enormously between LEAs. Many services consist only of a few advisory teachers, usually to cover the low incidence problems of vision, hearing and physical disability. In other LEAs, services exist to support pupils with Statements. LEA Services can give advice on general learning difficulties or behaviour management.

Child health services
Every LEA will be in a District Health Authority, but this may well not overlap geographically. Health Authority personnel availability may vary, but there will be a community paediatrician and health clinics where health

visitors, school nurses and speech and language therapists can be found. Local hospitals will also have a paediatric service in which physiotherapists and occupational therapists work. Just how much hospital services can work with schools varies enormously from district to district. There may also, in some areas, be child and adolescent mental health services or child guidance clinics.

For the school, the key health worker is often the school nurse who is part of the school health service. Through this nurse, the school doctor, therapists and other health professionals can be reached. If necessary, a special medical can be requested, if an SEN is suspected. It is essential to consult health records; to check that hearing and vision, for example, have been examined. The school health service will have records of all school aged children, although sometimes access is not easy. It may be best to ask the child's parent what tests have been done recently.

Pupils on regular medication for conditions such as asthma, diabetes or epilepsy do not have special educational needs as such, but their condition may be the cause of some schooling being missed. Certain pupils may have appliances that need to be maintained. An obvious example is hearing aids, which are usually checked by the LEA's hearing impaired service, who work in close co-operation with the health authority. Children with more severe disabilities will have been identified in early childhood by the health authority and the LEA will have been notified. The school nurse is the best source of information for schools. 'Health authorities must give parents a) information on the full range of local statutory services that might help them, and b) the names of voluntary organisations that might be of assistance when they consider a child under 5 may have SEN' (Revised Code of Practice, 10.4).

Social services

Each Local Authority will have a social service department which has a children's section and usually a section for those with disabilities. It has not been particularly easy in the past, for schools to make contact with social services on anything but a direct referral over single cases. 'Social services departments should designate an officer or officers who are responsible for working with schools and LEAs on behalf of children with SEN and to whom schools and LEAs should refer for advice' (Revised Code of Practice, 10.6).

Agencies whose focus is not the school

Certain agencies do not see schools as their clients or as a priority. Social services, in particular, focus on the family, but so do Child Guidance services (usually jointly run by health and education). It may be difficult for schools to access these services even for information, although teachers are sometimes invited to case conferences.

Connexions service

This is a new service to be set up in all LEAs to work with young people between the ages of 13 and 19. Its purpose is to provide guidance and support through teenage years and into adult life to those identified as having a special educational need.

Voluntary organisations

Many disability groups have charities that concentrate on one impairment. The longest standing are organisations like the Royal National Institute for the Blind (RNIB) and SCOPE (formally the Spastics Society); all of these have set up specialist schools and training for specialist teachers. There are now large numbers of other groups specialising in a wide range of disabilities. One of the key roles of voluntary organisations is to put parents in touch with others in the same situation as themselves. This, combined with factual information about the disability, is the most important way voluntary organisations can be used. The Council for Disabled Children in London publishes lists and contact numbers and can answer questions about a whole range of children's problems. There are also local generic groups supporting parents and children with all types of SEN. Local addresses should be available from Schools Psychological Services (SPS) or the LEA Parent Partnership Officer. These have now been appointed in most LEAs. Your school's SENCO may also have a list of local groups to which parents may be referred (see Useful Addresses).

Parents as part of the multi-professional network

Parents need to know about outside services and agencies and have their various roles explained especially if there is multi-agency involvement. Again this is best done informally, before the parent has to face a room full of strangers at an Annual Review or a case conference.

Parents themselves will often be the teacher's best source of information. In very complex cases the child may be known to up to 30 or so professionals. So for very complex disability cases the parent often is the 'key worker' for their child, linking the therapies and advice together into an individual plan. Other parents will be confused by the various agencies and may need the school's support in choosing appropriately. Notes will be kept by each service in their files, but it is the parent who has the total picture. In cases where, for example, three therapists require programmes of practice at home, there may not be time for the 'just ten minutes' practice from school as well.

Purposes of contributions from outside services and agencies
Staff from the education service can offer general advice and support to teachers on:

- the Code of Practice procedures of assessment and planning of IEPs; their reviews including communication with parents; support in developing the school's policy for SEN;
- teaching techniques and strategies to aid differentiation and modification at classroom level of the National Curriculum. This can be at all stages of the Code and should be seen as preventative, aiming at reducing numbers on the SEN register;
- managing support effectively at school and classroom levels; helping develop good support policies.

They also may offer consultative services to groups of staff to increase their confidence in a problem solving approach to meeting SEN. All of the above can contribute to school effectiveness in managing SEN at school-based stages, in particular staff from all services contribute advice to the Statement procedure.

Staff from Health and the Education Services have a statutory duty to:

- support parents and families, particularly at school-based stages. Support to parents may include helping those with attendance problems;
- give advice and support to pupils with a range of disabilities;
- provide direct therapies (speech and language, occupational or physiotherapy) or specialist support or teaching including provision and use of specialist equipment, ICT etc. For this to be effective, advice needs to contribute to classroom practice and access to the National Curriculum;
- contribute to case conferences and Annual Reviews of pupils.

Referrals to outside services
From the above it is clear that, as part of their SEN policy, schools need to develop their procedures for referrals and requests to support services and agencies. Where there are a number of possible choices, decisions

need to be made about the best route for support and advice. Over-referral to a number of agencies at one time, for the same case, is ineffective and wasteful of scarce resources.

It is also important in school to keep a record of who has been asked to help for any one child. This should be part of the paperwork attached to the IEP. Good practice is to have a top sheet in each file listing outside agency involvement and dates and indicating if a report is attached. Such a top sheet would provide a cumulative record. Communication within the school about referrals is vital, especially when, in secondary schools, some services are used by the pastoral systems and others by the learning support department.

The Revised Code points out that teachers should be very clear why they need external assistance. There would normally be a lack of expertise within the range that can be offered by the staff of a mainstream school, before further help is sought.

Support by giving advice on strategies

The overwhelming demand from teachers when seeking outside advice and support, is for strategies to meet individual targets and this within the structure of a normal school day and the National Curriculum. Some services that may be thought excellent for assessment do not directly support teachers. They may help tease out any within-child factors, e.g. medical reasons for a problem. These services may be either from the medical professions or may be working on a 'medical model' even from within education. But an understanding of the curriculum and the social context of the classroom and school is also needed if staff are to be fully supported in meeting the needs of more complex individuals.

Equipment and resources

Schools may need to borrow equipment for a short time to try it out and teachers will need training about how it should be used. If equipment is given with no training, it may just sit in a cupboard for most or all of the time. ICT, in particular, can help so many pupils with SEN, but knowing what equipment to buy and whether it will fit the pupil, requires the advice of an expert. In some areas an ICT/SEN expertise is available through learning support or advisory services. There are also a limited number of regional centres (see Useful Addresses).

Services working collaboratively with teachers

There are a number of puzzling pupils for whom it is not quite clear what is needed. Often the best way to support them will be to work with teachers rather than pupils to enhance the teacher's professional skills in managing all the pupils and their classes. If a visiting professional can find time for a joint problem solving session with a group of staff, together they can elicit the information already known and produce questions which then can be followed up in assessment. This will give staff strategies to try themselves, as well as directing focus onto the type of further information needed and from whom it could be expected.

Therefore, services will be at their most effective if they can be seen to increase the school's capacity for meeting SEN. This means services must meet teachers' as well as children's needs. If a teacher feels supported by knowledge that she/he is doing the right thing and can see the pupil taking a full part in school life and making progress, this will have been a piece of effective support. If, on the other hand, the expert advice has puzzled, confused or deskilled the teacher, the support will be worse than useless; it could be harmful.

The overarching purpose should be to support the teacher to support the child. The above applies to working with parents, for although school support services cannot focus on the parents' adult needs, they can support parents in supporting their children.

Chapter 7
Working with pupils and parents

The Code of Practice and the Green Paper and its Programme for Action all encourage teachers to see the importance of working with parents and in trying to establish a good partnership in order to support the child.

The rights of children to have their voices heard and their views considered is also affirmed by these publications.

Understanding pupil perspectives

For teachers to understand the pupil's own view of their learning and their experiences in school requires an ability on behalf of the teacher to change perspective. Teachers have to let go of their position of authority for a short time and view the world of the classroom from the pupil's point of view. This may best be done through becoming a careful observer for certain times and taking very detailed notes. If someone else can manage the class for a short session while this observation takes place, it may be easier to be free to observe.

Learning the skills: observation

Accurate observation for as little as ten minutes, if focused and prepared, can give some insights into a particular area of concern, whether for an individual pupil or a group. Remember that your observation could be biased so get a second opinion, for example, from an LSA where possible.

Learning observation skills gives teachers a useful tool for assessment and general problem solving. Observation can be for set times or of specific events or of a specific context, such as the playground. Starting the observation without a precise focus may be possible, but increasingly focusing in on an intended feature may give more insight. If pupil perspectives are the focus, this may need to be combined with interview techniques.

Using interviews and questionnaires

Another way to get a pupil's perspective is, of course, to ask the pupil to talk about or express their views in some way. This can be by direct questions about an aspect of their work, such as reading or homework, or it can be more open-ended questioning about school and their friends. Open-ended interviewing is difficult for some teachers to do, partly because of time constraints, partly because it is a skill to be learnt.

Sometimes LSAs may fare better, because they may offer less threat to pupils, or have time to see pupils in a more relaxed environment.

Another way is to give the whole class a questionnaire to evaluate an aspect of their own learning, possibly to give ratings about how confident they feel about various aspects of their learning. For younger pupils, faces with different expressions can be used to rate answers instead of words.

More difficult situations occur when the pupil lacks the language to express their thoughts and feelings in words. In these cases observations from more than one adult may need to be combined to give a feel for the pupil's perspective. Ancillary helpers' and parents' observations about different aspects of the pupil's development and feelings of self-worth are very helpful in putting together a joint perspective. If video cameras and tape recorders are used, this can help collect valuable data in cases where more direct questioning is difficult, for example, the developmentally young or pupils with language impairment. These would not be kept as a long-term record, but might help analyse complex observations.

Drawings and symbolic representations of situations as perceived during play can all add to the teacher's understanding of pupil perspectives.

School policy taking pupil perspectives into account

The Code of Practice emphasises the benefits of involving the child in assessment and intervention. These benefits are:

- Practical – children have important and relevant information. Their support is crucial to the effective implementation of any individual education programme.
- Principle – children have a right to be heard. They should be encouraged to participate in decision-making about provision to meet their special educational needs.

(Code of Practice, 1994, para. 2:35)

'Participation in education is a process that will necessitate all children being given the opportunity to make choices and understand that their views matter' (Revised Code of Practice, 2000, para. 3.4).

It will help if the school develops procedures for regularly taking note of pupil perspectives. Regular conferencing times when pupils' views are taken down, may be available for all pupils. The Records of Achievement approach to recording progress, as part of the school's assessment policy, will enhance the work for those working in special needs. The IEP review must include the pupil's perspective on their targets and their general feelings about making progress.

71

Working in partnership with parents

Parents are defined under the Children Act 1989 as those who have parental responsibility for the child or who have care of the child. Over the last two decades, legislation has increased parents' rights in relation to schools, choices and information.

Just as understanding the pupils' viewpoints needed a change of perspective for the teacher, so often does understanding the parents' viewpoint. If a true partnership with parents is to be established, then the teacher needs to learn to listen to and value the parents' expertise about their own child or their concerns about his or her progress. Parents may have insights into why their child finds learning difficult.

To do this effectively, it may be necessary to learn new skills. Teachers are good at expressing themselves and activating ideas. They may not be quite as good as listeners. Listening effectively is a skill to be learnt and practised.

Learning listening skills

When becoming a listener there are certain ground rules:

- keep eye contact;
- keep still, do not distract the person who is speaking by fiddling with pens etc.;
- keep your own comments to a minimum, such as 'I see', 'Right', 'I understand' and 'Yes'. If longer comments are required, make these reflective, i.e. feed back the main point as you understood it, so it can be checked. Use these comments to summarise the points and check you have understood what was said;
- do not be afraid to feed back feelings as well as facts. 'That must have made you angry', 'You were upset by ...'

Such listening sessions will need time limits, so these should be set up in advance if possible – 'We've got half an hour, – please tell me your concerns, worries ... and we will try to find some answers to the problems.' Check that the parent is happy for you to take notes. Often it is not a good idea to do this if you are really trying to listen, as you cannot keep eye contact and write notes. An alternative is to make time to summarise at the end of the session and agree a few points which can be written down. Establishing a feeling of trust is more important than note taking at this point. Once the problem has been identified and the parent feels they have been listened to, it will be possible to move into decision making.

Helping the parent to contribute in problem solving
As a first step, this requires that the problem has been clearly identified. Next, actions can be jointly planned with the parent to try to solve the problem. Problem solving again needs a sensitive approach from the teacher, while setting boundaries for what is achievable in school within limited resources. Wherever possible, the parents will feel more of a partner if they can suggest ideas to be discussed, perhaps offer to help in some way at home or in school. Joint targets can then be set and a date to review progress made. Copies of written notes of meetings should be given to parents wherever possible. As Cowne (2000) states:

'If schools have listened to parents when developing other policies, then parents' perspectives will already be reflected. Parents of pupils with SEN are however particularly vulnerable. Parents of children with difficulties and disabilities may lack confidence themselves, may even feel guilty (unjustifiably) about their child. Such parents are not always confident enough to ask for these views to be taken into account or to even know their rights. It is therefore essential that the school gives parents information about their rights. Parents need to have the assessment procedure explained. They need to know about LEA services which may be called on to support their child. School provision for SEN needs to be explained also.'

(p.84)

There are a few parents, however, who seem to have all too much confidence and knowledge of their rights. Such parents can pose a threat to some teachers. To build a partnership with these parents requires skills of assertiveness, ability to set limits for discussions and to know when to refer parents to the SENCO or head teacher.

Such parents can appear aggressive, even rude. Their feelings of anger, guilt and frustration over finding their child is not making expected progress, can be let loose on an unsuspecting and caring teacher, with the result that instead of a partnership, a confrontation occurs. As Dale (1996) explains, parents can go through a 'psychic shock' when they first hear of their child's disability. The first phase may only last a day or so, at which time they need sympathy and understanding. The next step will be to use a problem-solving approach to help parents come to terms with the new situation. This situation is, of course, best avoided by preventative strategies. Empathic listening skills can help establish a rapport followed by a problem-solving session. If the parent feels they really have been listened to and their viewpoints taken into account, they may be able to calm down and look for joint practical situations. If, however, their feelings seem irrational and solutions are beyond the resources of the school, it may be necessary to get help either from other members of the school; the head teacher or the SENCO, for example, or outside professionals such as an educational psychologist.

Almost all parents can be brought into a partnership situation even if only in small ways. Difficulties arise when promises are broken, resources lent do not come back to school, or the pupil is absent intermittently or for long periods. In many of these cases the teacher's motivation to work positively dwindles and possibly so does the parent's. It is sometimes difficult to keep the child's interests central to the problem solution. It is important to keep a record of interviews with parents. Often teachers state that they *did* talk to pupils and parents and yet there is no record of this on file. It is important to make a few notes after interviews with pupils and parents, recording viewpoints accurately where possible and dating your record. It helps teachers to keep records if there are procedures laid down by the school or if pro formas have spaces to record both pupil's views and parent's perspectives.

The Revised Code in the chapter on working in partnership with parents lays out the roles and responsibilities of LEAs, schools and the voluntary sector.

In the school section it is made clear that 'Schools should accept and value the contribution of parents and encourage participation' (p.12).

School policies in dealing with complaints

The Code of Practice states that the school SEN policy must include a section on how complaints will be dealt with. The policy should make clear to parents and children with SEN how they can make a complaint about the provision made for their child at the school and how that complaint will subsequently be dealt with by the school.

Schools usually have a general complaints system, but will need to give particular attention to SEN complaints. Often it is to the class teacher or the SENCO that the parent first turns. If the matter can be dealt with easily and quietly, this is best. It should be kept clearly in mind that the head teacher has the final responsibility for the school along with the governors. It is important, therefore, that procedures are clearly set out and published and not left to chance.

Chapter 8
Record keeping and transitions

For children with SEN careful, detailed record keeping of assessments, strategies and progress is essential. A great deal of information will be collected about some individuals, so it is important to select carefully what will be kept on file. Confidentiality is also an issue. Health services, for example, may not give access to their records yet some health information should be available to teachers. If parents give schools personal information this must be handled with discretion and confidentiality preserved.

Availability and content of records

It is important that records are passed on and used by teachers in the next class or school. For pupils who are transient this can be difficult. Those who move between schools frequently are at risk of not having their needs met due to poor transfer of information. What is transferred must be meaningful to the pupil's next teacher. Information such as National Curriculum records, Code of Practice stages and IEP details will enable a structure to be maintained. The sorts of areas to be covered are:

- which difficulties are current, and which are newly developed or are diminishing in importance;
- what strategies have been used and how effective they have been;
- how these fit into the broader developmental picture;
- what advice has been sought, from whom and with what result?

Good record keeping will also note:

- information about the pupil's learning styles;
- relationships with peers and adults;
- relevant information from parents about the pupil in the home context;
- the pupil's attitudes to learning, for example can they risk failure?
- observation about the pupil's strengths which can be used to build better self-esteem;
- suggestions as to how this pupil can be helped to function more effectively within the class;
- pupils' own views of their learning and relationships in school.

Transitions

Transition has at least two meanings in the context of special needs. The first is a general one that relates to the process of transition from home to nursery, nursery to primary, primary to secondary and so on. The second relates specifically to the Transition Plan required by the Code of Practice in Year 9 and in subsequent years until the young person leaves school.

Early Years

Prior to the age of two, special needs identification involves a process subject to Local Authority procedures. Disabilities are usually identified through the observations of parents/carers and through some aspect of health provision, for example, Health Visitors, or through the Social Services. A referral via a Local Authority 'under fives panel' may be another route. This panel usually consists of multi-agency professionals working with under fives across the Health, Education and Social services.

Depending on the nature of the need, which may be physical, developmental or learning-based, a range of developmental programmes may be put in place. These may include Portage schemes, developmental play or specific programmes linked to particular playgroups. For those involved in the co-ordination and organisation of this support the most obvious need is for clear records and consistent, clear communications between the parties involved. The possibility that the family may move during the period of support needs to be borne in mind.

Further considerations revolve around the parents' need for support, perhaps because of second language issues, particularly in dealing with different agencies and the involvement of their respective personnel, and the child's progress through the various developmental milestones. The location, access to and nature of the records kept during this support are crucial.

Pre-school provision

The attendance of a child at pre-school provision means significant changes for parents/carers and the rest of the family which are important for parents in general, but which may bring extra pressures for those whose children have special needs. Supporting parents at this stage with clear information, informal and welcoming contact procedures, and easy access to both the institution and staff involved are crucial. Good planning can ease transitions and make for a good start at school.

The sort of areas that need to be considered on entry will include:

- physical health and sensory functions;
- aspects of communication;
- motor development;
- self-organisation skills;
- development of social skills;
- emotional development as apparent in interactions with others;
- responses to learning activities.

The Revised Code has a chapter on Early Years Identification and Assessment. It encourages the graduated response with the two stages Early Years Action and Early Years Action Plus. It suggests that a SENCO be appointed for a group of Early Years Provisions whose role will be to liaise with parents and other practitioners and ensure IEPs are in place where appropriate. In all cases background information about children with SEN must be collected, recorded and updated.

Transfer to primary school and within the primary phase
There are important issues about entry to school for these more vulnerable children. Arrangements need to be flexible and offer a gradual entry into the full-time experience of school life. For example, it may help if the child can come for only part of the day or perhaps not go into the playground with all the older children. This may ease the shock of being with large numbers of bigger children. Ancillary helpers are of great importance in easing in these young children. Parents have a vital role to play in this planned entry.

This means certain children without Statements may need to be recorded as needing School Action on arrival. It will mean that an IEP is in place from entry to school. Such planning should help to build on what has already been done and help make a smooth transition to school. It is therefore essential that good use is made of pre-school records in planning to build on existing achievements. There must be no reluctance on behalf of teachers to read and use any records and information available from all sources including information from parents.

Clear explanations of why particular approaches are being discussed or particular agencies are being involved need to be uppermost in the minds of those organising consultations between parents and professionals. The accessibility of all that is discussed and its implications are critical if parents/carers are to be able to participate as equals in the ensuing consultations.

These issues remain current during the child's attendance at primary school and, where there is a Statement, are particularly important during interim and Annual Reviews and around the times of Key Stage assessments. The strategic concerns in this type of transition are to anticipate the needs and anxieties that will arise and to support a child's transition to the secondary phase or to other schools while in the primary phase.

Transfer to secondary school

The learning environment in secondary schools is different from primary settings in many ways. For example, in the primary school, the child has a much clearer idea of what is expected by his/her teacher. In a primary school most lessons are taught by the class teacher; in the secondary school the pupil is taught by many different teachers who will not be as familiar with their special educational needs.

There is more movement around the school which may put the pupil with some SEN at a disadvantage because they will have to carry and organise their equipment. Therefore, the planning for pupils transferring to secondary schools must be very carefully executed. Visits should be made to acclimatise the pupil to the new building and some of the teachers, especially the SENCO. Records must be transferred early enough in the summer term for those who need to know about the pupil's individual needs.

It is good practice when a pupil is transferring to another school for information to be provided so that the receiving school can plan provision in time. For pupils with a Statement, the Year 5 Annual Review should include transition planning to secondary schools.

For pupils with a range of SEN, planned transfer between schools is essential. The school organising the departure needs to make personal contact with the new school wherever possible, but should always make sure all records, including SEN records, are up to date and sent on in good time. A planning meeting, either at an Annual Review for a pupil with a Statement, or an IEP review for others, should include parents and if possible someone from the new school. Support services have a vital role in transition by helping the new school make plans. Often, the same support teacher may be able to work with the pupil in the new school, but even when this is not possible another member of their team may do so. The receiving school must read all records in good time so that plans are in place before entry, especially for the more vulnerable pupils. This is usually well done for those with sensory or physical disabilities. Support services and health personnel typically plan what equipment is needed and discuss mobility issues. Planning for pupils with more general difficulties is often much weaker. Yet for these pupils poor preparation may result in a setback to learning or in extreme cases such a traumatic start to the new school that the pupil never settles. In some schools members of the learning support department visit all tutor groups in the first two weeks of the new school year, in order to meet pupils with SEN and draw up a 'pen picture' of those learning characteristics which all staff need to know.

Transition Plans at 14+ for pupils with Statements

Under Part 3 of the Education Act 1996 and the Code of Practice (1994), LEAs have duties at the first Annual Review after the young person's 14th birthday to carry out a review to be repeated annually until school leaving, which must include a Transition Plan. The Revised Code strengthens the role of the school in running Annual Reviews and writing Transition Plans.

The Connexions service (see below) as well as those from education, health and social services who have been involved with the young person must be invited to attend the Annual Review. Information should be passed to relevant further education establishments. Parents' and young people's views must be sought.

Russell (1995) states that the challenge of the Transition Plan lies in development of continuity of assessment, review and programme planning from school through further educational, vocational and personal preparation for a valued and productive adult life.

For this to be successful there will need to be:

- co-ordination of the many different agencies and professions which can contribute to this process;
- the creation of positive approaches to participation by students and parents in assessment and planning for transition;
- the transfer of information and expertise between phases and agencies involved in transition;
- the provision of advocacy and advice directly to young people at a time of major changes in their family life and educational experience.

The Code of Practice (1994), paragraph 6:59 makes it very clear that the views of the young person should be actively involved in the development of the Transition Plan. As Gascoigne (1995) points out, this may be the first time that the young person is consulted without parents being present. She suggests that parents may find this period very stressful as their feelings are ambivalent. 'On the one hand they want their child to become as independent as possible, and on the other, they wish to extend their protection of them' (p.138). Both Gascoigne and Russell emphasise how sensitive parents can be and how much support they will need from those working with them.

Transition Plans should start in Year 9 and continue annually until the young person leaves school. It is important that all professionals involved build good relationships with the young person and their families and give them all information about what is available in their local area.

The Connexions service

This is a new service which will work with all young people between the ages of 13 and 19. The LEA must set up this service to provide guidance on careers and services. A Personal Advisor from the Connexions service should attend the Year 11 Annual Review in order to ensure the Transition Plan is updated appropriately for those pupils with a Statement.

Schools also need to build links to local further education colleges. Sometimes link provision can be arranged to give opportunities for integration into the adult environment of further education. The Government promises to strengthen the guidance in the revised Code of Practice to underline the importance of the transition processes.

Communication

Good communication between everyone involved with children and young people with SEN is vital. It includes keeping records which are accessible to those who might need them. This means regular reviewing of paperwork, seeing that it is up to date and relevant. Good communication also means sharing decision making and involving pupils and parents in the process.

Chapter 9
Integration or inclusive education?

The Warnock Report in 1978 discussed the principle of educating handicapped and non-handicapped children together. This was described as 'integration' in Britain and 'mainstreaming' in America.

The Warnock Report states that:

'It had always been a general policy that no child should be sent to a special school who could be satisfactorily educated in an ordinary one.'

(p.99)

The Warnock Report described three types of integration. These were:

- locational
- social
- functional.

Locational integration related to the proximity of special and mainstream provision who might share the same site and possibly organising planned times when children visited both types of school.

Social integration related to situations where special classes were sited in mainstream schools and children shared out-of-classroom activities such as eating together and playtime. This gave opportunities for those with disabilities to develop easy relationships with non-disabled peers.

Functional integration described children with disabilities attending mainstream school, either full time or part time, but taking part in all the normal activities of their class.

The emphasis on all these types was still on the individual child being able and ready to take part in the mainstream activities. The 1981 Act built on these principles by stating that wherever possible, children with special needs should be educated in mainstream schools. In America, this was often described as educating in the least restrictive environment.

In the period after the 1981 Act, there was a move to integrate many types of disabled pupils into the mainstream, most often those with physical or sensory impairment.

Over the years between 1981 and 1994 when the Code of Practice was published, there was an increase in 'mainstreaming' both nationally and internationally. Most LEAs had cut special provision and tried not to send pupils to residential special schools unless essential.

Norwich (1996) suggested that one way of conceptualising SEN is to see this label as a way of describing the inability of the mainstream to include and provide for a diversity of learners.

If this perspective is encouraged this leads away from the concept of integrating individual children from special provision to one where schools are encouraged to widen their inclusiveness and flexibility in meeting an ever-widening range of diversity.

Integration or inclusion?

Integration was the term used from the Warnock Report up to 1998 to describe the placement of pupils with SEN in mainstream or ordinary schools. Some of these pupils may have started their schooling in special schools and then been 'integrated' on a part-time or full-time basis. Increasingly, however, pupils with SEN were already in the mainstream either with or without a Statement. There has been an increase in the number of pupils in mainstream schools with Statements over the last decade. However, there has not necessarily always been a corresponding reduction in numbers of pupils in special schools. This varies from LEA to LEA, however, depending on local policies and provision. This really means that more children are receiving a Statement of SEN than was the case when the 1981 Act was passed. In other words, the level of integration may not really have changed significantly.

The challenge is very great to those planning for a range of children which may include very able pupils and pupils with serious disabilities. It is therefore not surprising one solution used in the past was to group pupils with similar needs, and perhaps teach them in different classes or even schools.

The 1997 Green Paper 'Excellence for All Children' and its subsequent Programme for Action (1998) state clearly that it is the Government's intention to see many more children with special educational needs in mainstream primary and secondary schools.

Since the Programme for Action Plan was published in 1998 the term 'inclusive education' has been used in preference to 'integration'. The focus has changed from preparing individuals to 'fit' mainstream schools to helping those schools change to be more inclusive by nature.

The Action Plan goes on to say that inclusion is a process – it may begin with placement in mainstream schools of those with SEN, but it continues by making the school one where these pupils' contributions are equally valued and where they take part in the full range of curriculum and social life of the schools.

The 1998 Action Plan promises to promote further inclusion by:

- requiring LEAs to publish information about their policy on inclusion in their Education Development Plans;
- reviewing the statutory framework for inclusion;
- identifying good practice by special schools and developing links with mainstream schools;
- ensuring children with special educational needs are treated fairly in school admission procedures;
- providing financial support through the Standards Fund by a grant given to LEAs for training.

However, as Rose (1998) points out,

'The Green Paper demonstrates a major significant weakness in that it fails to address the fact that many schools are as yet unable and, in a number of instances, unprepared to promote an appropriate curriculum model which will encourage inclusion.'

(p.28)

Ainscow (1997) points out that integration and inclusion are different concepts. He describes inclusive education as starting with the assumption that all children have the right to attend their neighbourhood school. Therefore, he says, 'the task becomes one of developing the work of the school as a response to pupil diversity. This has to include a consideration of overall organisation, curricular and classroom practice and support for learning and staff development' (p.5).

Lindsay (1997) points out that there are many dilemmas with regard to disability and values. He reminds us that there is a position which accords positive value to a person with a disability as a moral and political right. Those campaigning for inclusion and the rights of the disabled might also remember that some groups (such as the deaf community) do not always want inclusive education as they interpret this as disintegration of deaf people's society.

Hornby (1999), in his review of published research on policies of inclusive education, points out that in the end it is the right of children and young people to an appropriate education that matters most. Integration into the adult community should be the long-term aim. Therefore he concludes decisions must be made taking account of the needs of each individual and each situation.

The change from an entitlement curriculum to an inclusive curriculum

In the years after the Education Reform Act announced the National Curriculum, there were few Government-led studies about what this meant for pupils with special educational needs. In 1988 and 1989 there was much discussion about exemption from the National Curriculum for pupils with special educational needs which was allowed by the Act and described in detail in Circular 22/89. In the event, exemptions were little used by schools, probably due to the complexity of procedures. In 1994 the Dearing Revision of the National Curriculum made these less necessary.

The entitlement to a normal mainstream curriculum is an essential element in inclusive education. It is important therefore to make this a practical reality, not just a rhetorical ideal. The 1988 Education Act was a significant milestone for pupils with special educational needs, because it gave an entitlement to a broad, balanced and relevant curriculum to all pupils. Although when it was first designed it did not address the needs of those pupils with special educational needs specifically, it was suggested that by use of differentiation, teachers would find ways of making the curriculum accessible to all.

O'Brien (1998) reminds us that the curriculum includes all elements of intended and unintended learning that occur in and through the school. He continues by saying that 'for the individual to become an active stakeholder in society, she or he must become an active stakeholder in the curriculum' (p.147).

Lewis (1995) also pointed out how the cross-curricular elements such as citizenship, so important in special schools, have been relatively neglected in mainstream schools. The new Revised National Curriculum (2000) gives even more emphasis to flexible planning and inclusive practice and should make it possible to address some of the issues.

The present drive to push up standards taken alongside the publishing of both primary and secondary league tables might be seen as counterproductive to the inclusive principles of the Programme for Action. Schools may find difficulty in giving equal value to pupils with SEN who make slow progress, but do not achieve the acquired national level of achievement in the statutory national tests.

Making your classroom more inclusive
- The first step will be to read the records of the pupils in your class and to get to know their strengths as well as those parts of the curriculum that cause their difficulties.

84

- The next step will be to carry out further observations or teacher assessments to complete any gaps in your knowledge of each child's achievements. At the same time you need to note the pupils' preferred learning styles and strategies. It is important to discuss these with the pupil. Even young children can tell you something about their preferences.
- Planning follows. Each lesson or scheme of work will need to be adapted to include the range of pupils in your class. It may largely be a matter of classroom and resource allocation. But it will also be important to consider the way you give instructions and the attitudes you portray when talking to the child.
- Working with peer groups. For a classroom to be 'inclusive' requires work with all the pupils so they can understand the difficulties some of their fellow pupils need to overcome. Certain disabilities such as limited vision, hearing or mobility need explanation. Equally, those who have difficulty with communication, poor attention span or low self-esteem require peer group understanding.
- Working with parents. Parents of pupils with SEN will need opportunities to share the success of their child as well as chances to tell of their anxieties. Developing a real equal partnership with parents takes time.

Getting help and training

Newly qualified teachers will benefit from being given opportunities to discuss appropriate teaching and classroom management strategies with experienced staff. Robertson (1999) suggests that newly qualified teachers should probably be given this support from SENCOs in their induction year. He warns that this may prove difficult when the already overloaded SENCO is asked to mentor a new teacher. He does feel that this may require a stronger commitment to induction training than there is at present.

Develop a team approach to curricular planning

Support is often the method of differentiation most often chosen for special educational needs work. Support can be conceptualised as support for the pupil, but also as curriculum support with the class teacher. Best practice is when support personnel and teachers work as a team. The team can be extended to include visiting specialists, such as peripatetic teachers and therapists for those with more complex needs. The role of this team is to be as creative as possible in integrating the special requirements of the individual into normal class delivery of the curriculum. Other pupils often enjoy doing activities or games which may originally have been designed for an individual.

Pickles (1998) reminds us that, 'Therapy should be seen as part of everyday living and the responsibility of the whole support team. Without this understanding there is a danger that therapy is seen as something "done" to the child to "make things better"' (p.5).

Some pupils will have additional resources to help them access the curriculum. Some of these are technical in nature. Equipment must be kept in good condition with spare parts and switches available. Pupils may need training to use it efficiently. For example, keyboard skills may need to be taught by a suitable instructor employed just for this purpose.

Celebrate diversity and recognise that the sum of the whole is greater than the part

The learning community of the classroom will support a wealth of diversity itself, if flexibly managed and democratically controlled. When pupils have joint purposes with teachers, they can carry forward individuals whose needs may be quite great and who on their own would struggle to make any progress.

We have a diverse population of children and young people in our schools. They vary in cultural background, aspirations, abilities and perspectives. Inclusiveness requires this diversity to be celebrated and developed. Inclusiveness means being flexible and open to a range of opportunities. This is one of the challenges of inclusive education.

Appendix
Case studies

Here are a few examples of case studies of pupils with Statements of special need. Each has a description of the child and some long-term targets to meet these needs.

Case Study One – Year 1

Ling is a 5 year-old girl of low ability whose special educational needs arise from developmental delay associated with physical disability (mild cerebral palsy).

Ling is highly distractible. She is restless and wilful. Her poor concentration impedes her learning across the curriculum. Ling has a poor grip, which makes holding pens and pencils difficult. Her self-care skills are progressing. She can dress and undress herself, except for her shoes. She feeds herself with adapted cutlery, but needs food cut up for her. Ling has an unsteady gait and can fall frequently. She wears a helmet for protection. She can sit on normal chairs, but may need a footrest.

Ling enjoys looking at books and having them read to her. She memorises words from her favourite stories and can recognise her name and those of her friends. Ling is friendly and chatty and is popular with others. She finds following rules difficult and her lack of concentration can affect her play activities. Ling is happy to work and is positive about herself.

The objectives for Ling should be for her to:

1. improve concentration span and focus on task;
2. improve hand grip and pencil control leading to early writing of letters and words;
3. continue to improve self-care skills – feeding and dressing;
4. continue to improve balance;
5. increase word recognition and early pre-reading skills;
6. learn to play co-operatively;
7. continue to build positive self-esteem and confidence.

Case Study Two – Year 3

Dan is an 8 year-old boy of below average ability whose special educational needs arise from general learning difficulties including language and literacy. Dan is unable to listen to the class teacher and to retain information or follow instructions. Dan's concentration is very poor and he is easily distracted, even in a small group situation. Dan has difficulties with his pro-prioceptive responses. He has problems with visual and touch perception and fine motor skills. His handwriting is poor and immature. Dan has very poor short-term memory. This is affecting all of his learning as he forgets instructions and much of what he has previously learnt, thus making the retention of mathematical concepts particularly difficult.

Dan has made a start at reading, he can read simple three-letter words and makes some attempts at decoding. Dan can write short stories with support, but his language structure is poor. Dan lacks confidence, but responds well to praise and encouragement. Dan is unsure of his boundaries. He is very easily influenced by his peer group, sometimes being led into unsuitable behaviours.

The objectives for Dan should be for him to:

1. improve concentration and attention span;
2. improve manipulative hand skills, such as the correct use of pencil and scissors;
3. improve basic number skills to a level more appropriate to his age and ability;
4. develop literacy skills to a level appropriate to his age and ability;
5. increase his self-esteem, confidence and motivation by ensuring success in the tasks that he can accomplish;
6. improve social skills and quality of interaction with peers.

Case Study Three – Year 5

Declan is a 10 year-old boy of average ability whose special educational needs arise from specific learning difficulties. His concentration span is short and his listening skills poor. He is reading at a 5-6 year-old level. Declan has recently increased his sight vocabulary and is looking for patterns in words. He has difficulty in finding meaning in the texts he reads. He has made recent improvements in spelling, now reaching a 7-8 year-old level. He is beginning to be more confident of medial vowels. It takes him a long time to think out spellings, resulting in a very slow writing speed. He has made progress in acquiring a joined-up writing script.

Declan's self-esteem is low and he is afraid of tackling work that may result in failure. He gives up easily and puts in very little effort. Declan finds it difficult to adapt to new teachers. He can be demanding of adult attention and is immature. Declan loses equipment and is poorly organised.

The objectives for Declan should be for him to:

1. improve listening skills and attention span;
2. continue to improve sight vocabulary, phonic awareness and reading for meaning;
3. continue to improve fluency in writing and spelling;
4. continue to improve number work, particularly problem solving;
5. increase initiative and learn to take more risks;
6. increase independence and self-organisation.

Here are a further set of studies of pupils on school-based stages of the Code of Practice. Try to write up to five targets for one of these which might be suitable for an IEP. It is probably wise to choose one for each area of concern, remembering however to build on the pupils' strengths.

Case Study Four – Year 1

Wayne is developmentally young and finds fitting into the class situation difficult. His speech and language are immature. He listens for short periods but finds following instructions hard and he is often to be found wandering around the class looking at others. He is willing to work in small group situations and responds to praise.

Case Study Five – Year 3

Jennifer has mild cerebral palsy affecting one side of her body. She walks with an unsteady gait. Her fine motor control is poor, affecting handwriting. Jennifer can read well and enjoys stories. Her understanding of number is good but she finds recording difficult. Jennifer is friendly and co-operative.

Case Study Six – Year 5

Lisa has literacy difficulties, particularly with spelling. She is making steady progress with reading and is beginning to enjoy stories. She is also finding aspects of mathematics difficult such as remembering sequences and the position of digits in tens and units. She finds telling the time hard, only recognising hours and half hours at present. Her self-esteem is improving and she responds well to praise.

Case Study Seven – Year 9

Zak has a moderate sensory neural hearing loss and wears post-aural hearing aids. In some classes he also uses a radio aid. Zak reads well and enjoys writing. He finds oral mathematics difficult and has difficulty with some concepts. His spoken vocabulary is reasonably good and his speech is intelligible and is usually fluent. He makes mistakes in spelling and with some words when doing free writing. He makes use of lip reading, so teachers must not stand with their back to the light.

Case Study Eight – Year 9

Connor is a 14 year-old boy who has difficulty in comprehending and making progress with the secondary curriculum. Connor has very low attainments in reading and mathematics. Progress has been very slow despite extra tuition. Connor has a positive attitude to learning. He concentrates well on appropriate work. Connor is friendly, generous and patient and has good peer relationships. Connor enjoys sport and physical education and other activities not requiring literacy ability.

References

Ainscow (1997) 'Towards inclusive schooling'. *British Journal of Special Education*. Vol. 24, No. 1, pp.3-6.

Armstrong, T. (1994) *Multiple Intelligences in the Classroom*. Virginia: ASCD.

The Basic Skills Agency (1997) 'A course for teachers of Key Stages 3 and 4'. London: The Basic Skills Agency.

Carpenter, B., Ashdown, R. & Bovair, K. (1996) *Enabling Access: Effective Teaching and Learning for Pupils with Learning Difficulties*. London: Fulton.

Chin, S. (1992) 'Individual Diagnosis and Cognitive Style', Miles, T. R. & Miles, E. (Eds) *Dyslexia and Mathematics*. Routledge: London and New York.

Cowne, E. A. (2000) *The SENCO Handbook: Working within a whole school approach*. London: Fulton.

Dale, N. (1996) *Working with Families with Special Needs: Partnership and Practice*. London: Routledge.

Daniels, H. (1996) 'Back to Basics: three R's for special needs education'. *British Journal of Special Education*. Vol. 23, No. 4.

Dearing, R. (1994) *The National Curriculum and its Assessment*. London: SCAA.

DECP (1999) 'Report by the working party of the Division of Educational and Child Psychology of the British Psychological Society'. BPS: Leicester.

DES (1978) *Special Educational Needs: Report of the Committee of Enquiry into the Education of Handicapped Children and Young People* (The Warnock Report). London: HMSO.

DES (1988) *Education Reform Act*. London: HMSO.

DfE (1981) *The Education Act*. London: HMSO.

DfE (1989) *Circular 22/89*. London: HMSO.

DfE (1994a) *The Code of Practice on the Identification and Assessment of Special Educational Needs*. London: HMSO.

DfE (1994b) *The Organisation of Special Education*. Circular 6/94. London: HMSO.

DfEE (1996) *The Education Act*. London: HMSO.

DfEE (1997) *Excellence for All Children: Meeting Special Educational Needs*. London: The Stationery Office Ltd.

DfEE (1998a) *Meeting Special Educational Needs: A Programme for Action*. London: The Stationery Office Ltd.

DfEE (1998b) *The National Literacy Strategy: A Framework for Teaching*. The Stationery Office Ltd.

DfEE (1998c) *The National Numeracy Strategy: A Framework for Teaching Mathematics*. The Stationery Office Ltd.

DfEE (1999) *Social Inclusion: Pupil Support*. Circular 10/99. The Stationery Office Ltd.

DfEE (2000) Draft Code of Practice and Guidance, ref. 0120/2000.

Fox, G. (1998) *Learning Support Assistants: teachers and assistants working together*. London: Fulton.

Gardner, H. (1993) *Frames of Mind: the theory of multiple intelligences*. Second edition. London: Fontana.

Gascoigne, E. (1995) *Working with Parents as Partners in SEN*. London: Fulton.

Gross, J. (1993) *Special Educational Needs in the Primary School: a practical guide*. Buckingham: Open University Press.

Hornby, G. (1999) 'Inclusion or delusion: can one fit all?' *Support for Learning*. Vol. 14, No. 4.

Lewis A. (1995) *Primary special needs and the National Curriculum.* Second edition. London: Routledge.

Lindsay, G. (1997) 'Values, Rights and Dilemmas'. *British Journal of Special Education.* Vol. 24, No. 2.

Miller, O. (1996) *Supporting Children with Visual Impairment in Mainstream Schools.* INPUT series. London: Franklin Watts.

Norwich, B. (1996) 'Special needs education or education for all: connective specialisation an ideological impurity'. *British Journal of Special Education.* Vol. 23, No. 3.

O'Brien, T. (1998) 'The Millennium Curriculum: confronting the issues and proposing solutions'. *Support for Learning*, Vol. 13, No. 4.

OFSTED (1999) *The Special Educational Needs Code of Practice: 3 years on – The contribution of individual education plans to the raising of standards for pupils with SEN.* London: HMSO.

Pickles, P. (1998) *Managing the curriculum for children with severe motor difficulties: a practical approach.* London: Fulton.

QCA (1999) *The Revised National Curriculum.* www.nc.uk.net

Robertson, C. (1999) 'Initial Teacher Education and Inclusive Schooling'. *Support for Learning*, Vol. 14, No. 4.

Rose, R. (1998) 'The Curriculum: a vehicle for inclusion or a lever for exclusion?' in *Promoting Inclusive Education.* London: Routledge.

Russell, P. (1995) 'The Transition Plan' in Discussion Papers IV, pp.57-65. *Schools' SEN Policy Pack.* London: National Children's Bureau.

Schools Curriculum Assessment Authority (1996) *Supporting pupils with SEN: Key Stage 3.* London: SCAA.

Seach, D. (1998) *Autistic Spectrum Disorder: Positive Approaches for Teaching Children with ASD.* Tamworth: NASEN.

Stevenson, R. & Palmer, J. (1994) *Principles, Processes and Practices*. London: Cassell.

TTA (1998) *National Standards for Special Educational Needs Co-ordinators*. TTA: London.

Thomas, G. (1992) *Effective Classroom Teamwork*. London: Routledge.

Tod, J., Castle, F. & Blamires, M. (1998) *Individual Education Plans: Implementing Effective Practice*. London: Fulton.

Vail, P. (1992) *Learning Styles. Modern Learning Press*. Rosemont: New Jersey.

Wragg, E. C. (1997) *The Cubic Curriculum*. London: Routledge.

Further Reading

Berger, A. & Gross, J. (1999) *Teaching the Literacy Hour in an Inclusive Classroom: Supporting pupils with learning difficulties in a mainstream environment*. London: Fulton.

Berger, A., Denise, M. & Portman, J. (2000) *Implementing the National Numeracy Strategy – For pupils with learning difficulties – Access to the Daily Mathematics Lesson*. London: Fulton.

DfEE (1998) *The National Literacy Strategy: Resources for supporting pupils with SEN during the Literacy Hour*.

Edwards, S. (1998) *Modern Foreign Languages for all – Success for pupils with Special Educational Needs*. Tamworth: NASEN.

El-Naggar, O. (1996) *Specific Learning Difficulties in Mathematics: A Classroom Approach*. Tamworth: NASEN.

Grove, N. (1998) *Literature for All: Developing Literature in the Curriculum for Pupils with Special Educational Needs*. London: Fulton.

Hall, D. (1995) *Assessing the Needs of Bilingual Pupils.* London: Fulton.

Henderson, A. (1998) *Maths for the Dyslexic – A Practical Guide.* London: Fulton.

Hinson, M. (Ed) (1999) *Surviving the Literacy Hour.* Tamworth: NASEN.

Kenward, H. (1996) *Physical Disabilities.* Tamworth: NASEN.

Lawson, H. (1998) *Practical Record Keeping – Development and resource material for staff working with pupils with special educational needs.* Second edition. London: Fulton.

Malone, G. & Smith, D. (1996) *Learning to Learn – Developing study skills with children who have special educational needs.* Tamworth: NASEN.

McNamara, S. & Moreton, G. (1997) *Understanding Differentiation – A Teachers Guide.* London: Fulton.

OFSTED (1999) *Principles into Practice: Effective Education for Pupils with Emotional and Behavioural Difficulties.* London: OFSTED Publications Centre (ref. HMI 177).

OFSTED (1999) *Pupils with specific learning difficulties in mainstream schools.* London: OFSTED Publications Centre (ref. HMI 208).

Spotlight on Special Educational Needs – Series. Tamworth: NASEN.

Thomas, G., Walker, D. & Webb, J. (1998) *The Making of the Inclusive School.* London: Routledge.

Tod, J. & Cornwall, J. (1998) *Emotional and Behavioural Difficulties: Individual Education Plans.* London: Fulton.

Wade, J. 'Including all learners: QCA's approach'. *British Journal of Special Education.* Vol. 26, No. 2.

Useful Addresses

Council for Disabled Children
C/o National Children's Bureau
8 Wakely Street
London EC1V 7QE
Tel: 020 7843 6000

CENMAC
Charlton Park School
Charlton Park Road
London SE7 8JB
Tel: 020 8854 1019
e-mail: cenmac@cenmac.greenwich.gov.uk

SEMERC
1 Broadbent Road
Water Sheddings
Oldham
Manchester OL1 4LB
Tel: 0161 627449
e-mail: info@semerc.demon.co.uk

RADAR
Royal Association for Disability & Rehabilitation
250 City Road
London EC1
Tel: 020 7250 3222

Contact-A-Family
170 Tottenham Court Road
London WIP OHA
Tel: 020 7383 3555

Parents in Partnership
Unit 2
Ground Floor
70 South Lambeth Road
London SW8 1RL
Tel: 020 7735 7733